THE FEMININE

spacious as the sky

SHAMBHALA   *1977*

THE FEMININE
spacious as the sky

MIRIAM & JOSÉ ARGÜELLES

Boulder & London

SHAMBHALA PUBLICATIONS, INC.
1123 Spruce Street
Boulder, Colorado 80302

ISBN 0-87773-113-6
LCC 77-6012

Distributed in the United States by Random House
and in Canada by Random House of Canada Ltd.

Distributed in the Commonwealth by Routledge & Kegan Paul Ltd.
London and Henley-on-Thames.

Printed in the United States of America.

To our parents

_____

Praise to the Mother of the Victorious One of all times,
Who is the Perfection of Discriminating Awareness
    inexpressible by words even if one attempted to speak,
Who is without origin and end, of the nature of celestial space,
And who is the sphere of transcending awareness
    which is experienced by and in ourselves.

from the *Prajnaparamita*

Contents

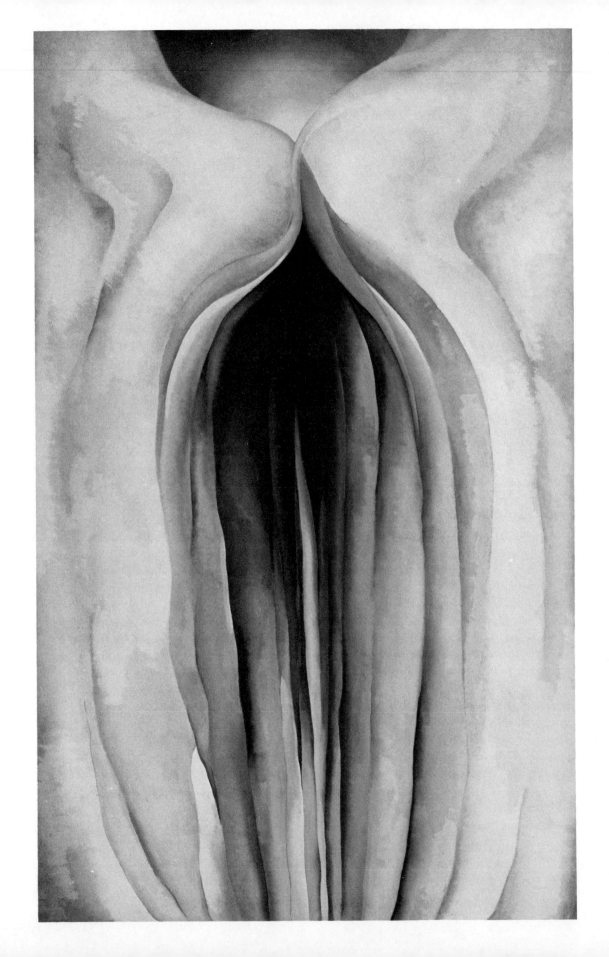

Introduction

THE FEMININE, spacious as the sky, has been a continuous inspiration in the unfolding of our own relationship and the way in which we view the world. Initially, the feminine was a diffusely felt energy that provided creative coherence to our decision, some ten years ago, to involve ourselves in mutual projects. While each of us naturally followed an individual direction and development, from time to time we would weave together our experiences into a collaborative effort.

The first step in our adventure was painting, through which we discovered the mandala as the visual form dynamically accommodating our energy. Behind the colors and images was a guiding intuition suggesting and leading us on to further areas of study and realms of the imagination. In *Mandala* (1972), we described a fundamental, nondual space as we understood it and as it is expressed in different spiritual and symbolic traditions.

As our own artistic explorations and research into cultural history developed, we were becoming more conscious of the intuitive and nonverbal potential with which the feminine is traditionally associated. At the same time, about five years ago, we began the practice of Buddhist meditation. The discipline of sitting meditation was literally a grounding that helped clarify our interests and provided a deepened awareness of the space accommodating and permeating our mind and actions. The space created by meditation seemed to have a fertile, feminine aspect manifesting in the capacity for the unceasing generation and dissolution of numberless emotions and thoughts. Inseparable from this fertility were glimpses of an intelligence experiencing the space of meditation.

Our seduction by the feminine was furthered by questions and issues raised by our growing family, as well as the women's movement, which made us acutely aware of the great residue of chauvinism within ourselves and extending through all levels of social and cultural life. A fundamental question presented itself: how were we to understand feminine and masculine as cosmic principles in relation to biological maleness and femaleness? If feminine and masculine are inseparable aspects of a whole, why was it that it was the feminine inviting us and providing the home ground in which to begin a more intensified and focused exploration?

1

1.   *Grey Line With Black, Blue and Yellow.* ca. 1923. Georgia O'Keeffe.

THE FEMININE   As soon as we articulated these questions, we discovered that there was no turning back. There was a labyrinthine and mirrorlike quality in accepting and using the terms feminine and masculine as expressions of our relation to the world. Despite our occasional impatience with and resistance toward each other's points of view, we kept discovering a space that allowed us to struggle with our ideas and that simultaneously nurtured an ever greater clarity. At one point, much to our amazement and amusement, we realized that the very process of trying to articulate the feminine was the play of the feminine itself.

As a man and woman writing a book on the feminine for men and women, we have grown increasingly sensitive to the richness of the interpersonal issues and the complexities of our common cultural heritage. The contents of this book are a weaving together of the primary experience of the feminine in everyday life situations and as reflected in the basic themes of spiritual traditions, myth, and history.

Through the long process of research, writing, drawing, and gathering the illustrations for this book, there are a few people who especially stand out and deserve our gratitude. Chögyam Trungpa, Rinpoche, who introduced us to the practice of meditation, has been an inspiration and critical force whose value cannot be estimated. Through Trungpa Rinpoche, we have come in touch with a living tradition and lineage of wisdom, whose practice nourishes the ground of our daily lives. We also express appreciation to: Khyentse Rinpoche and Dudjom Rinpoche, who offered their time in listening to and clarifying basic questions; Sam Bercholz whose confidence and vision remained constant, invigorating us when we needed it the most; Carolyn Rose King whose interest in and unflagging critical attention to our work imbued us with a greater sense of precision and quality; and to Fred Kline of the Asian Art Museum, San Francisco, who openly gave of his time and knowledge. There are many others who helped and inspired, each in his own way, but several deserve special tribute: Dr. James Sacamano, who provided us with wit and warmth; and most of all, our two children, Joshua and Tara, whose patience and love far exceed their years.

Miriam and José Argüelles
Boulder, Colorado
July 1977

2. Northwest Coast Indian totem pole, symbolizing ceaseless generation from infinite space.

CHAPTER ONE

The Matrix of the Unborn

THERE IS NOTHING that does not have a mother. Anything in the world, whether an idea, a living being, or a form of nature, has been generated from another idea, being, or form. This generative process goes back indefinitely, causing one to ask: who or what is the first mother? What is the ultimate mother of the world and universe with its wide range of forms, animate and inanimate? In trying to return to the beginning of the beginning, and even to go back to before the beginning of the beginning, one is confronted with a paradox: *whatever lies beyond the mother of the first mother is beyond all concept.* Every reasonable notion of time and space dissolves into a primordial pool that seems unfathomable. One is unable to imagine this beginningless beginning. Yet because something is beyond conceptualization does not mean that it is invalid or unreal.

Trying to find a beginning cannot always be thought about or discovered logically. One encounters instead an experience that leaps beyond logic and language; that is simultaneously empty and open. As children, many of us probably questioned the origins of existence. It may have occurred while gazing up at the sky or contemplating a growing tree. The child wonders where the first seed of the tree came from; where the sky may end; if there are other universes beyond this one. At one point in these imaginative unravelings, there may come a moment of exhilaration where the question turns into a statement: however remote, the beginning before the beginning, or the end beyond the end, does exist. This search for a definite starting point is like peeling an onion, removing layer after layer, until one finally reaches the center where nothing resides except the same empty space that surrounds and maintains the entire onion.

Today our largest telescopes can encompass over one hundred million galaxies of which our Milky Way is but one. The enormity in stellar mass and interstellar distance of the universe, although finite, is almost incalculable. According to a widely accepted contemporary astrophysical theory, this immense universe exploded from and probably will collapse back into an infinitesimal point with a radius of virtually zero (less than 10^{-33} cm.) and a density so great that it exceeds all possible measurement. The origin of the present universe is rationally and logically inconceivable. Somehow it just happened—the Big Bang! What preceded the Big Bang is itself beyond all conception, and the possibility arises that our universe is beginningless, preceded by other universes without origin.

What lies beyond the first mother, whether we search our own experience or the vastness of the physical universe, still seems to be a kind of mother, something that accommodates all possible questions and sustains the birth and death of ideas and living beings. This mother of all things is groundless, without any identifiable source. Whether attempting to comprehend genesis biologically, astrophysically, or mythologically, a point beyond any concept of time and space is inevitably reached. Here, preceding the discernible beginning, there is an indefinable space that nevertheless possesses tremendous fertility. Without this originless fecundity, the whole cosmological process would not have begun. This primordial, all-accommodating spaciousness is the fundamental quality of the feminine.

Without maker or producer, without having a mother of its own, the feminine is unborn. Though it was never conceived and remains inconceivable, the feminine still can be experienced, simply because it is. The word unborn creates a certain arrest in one's thinking, for upon first considering it, one may think that unborn means the opposite of born, describing a condition of never coming into fruition or actualization, or of remaining in a state of suspended, pregnant animation. However, the unbornness of the feminine is a fertile situation that is neither tentative nor negative.

Instead, the unborn quality of the feminine provides an expanded dimension in which to understand "the born." Describing a process that has a beginning and an end, a birth and a death, what is born is by nature conditioned and relative. Whatever is born exists precariously, being vulnerable to accident, sickness, old age, and ultimately death. However, this entire process of change, birth, death, and impermanence is permeated and supported, preceded and followed, by an unborn environment of unceasing fertility.

The understanding of the feminine as the unborn container of creation and destruction may arise from a personal consideration of birth and bornness, one's own transitory existence. "Here I am, born into this world in this particular body. Was there something, or was I something, before I was born? Will I be anything after I die? Is everything that I am inherited from my

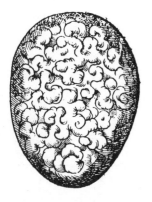

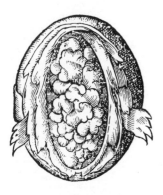

4.

parents and ancestors?'' One approach to answering these questions may be to seek the roots of one's birth by constructing a geneological tree of ancestors. One may eventually reach the point where one's historical predecessors become indistinct, lost in the patterns of branches and roots. No matter whether one uses a literal or symbolic approach, the search for one's ancestry or origins

5. Aztec Earth Goddess.

eventually becomes blurred, and then the possibility arises of seeing the evanescent quality of one's life and family history, like glimpsing a fish suddenly leaping out of the water and just as quickly disappearing. The myriad forms of the phenomenal world are, in this way, continually rising and falling, coming into and going out of existence. From where are they rising and to where are they falling? This *where* is the unceasing and all-accommodating space of the unborn.

7

Not only is one continually experiencing an infinite variety of passing phenomena, but each person's experience seems to be different. Besides having a particular fixed version of or attitude about one's experience, one may find that even this attitude can change from day to day. However unique a given experience and however many different versions of the world there are, human beings still share aspects of the world that transcend environment. Each of us lives and relates with the fundamental energies of life and death, creation and destruction. Each of us is involved with the start, growth, and decay of one thing and the emergence of another, whether it is the pattern of a love affair, the development of an idea from a blueprint into actuality, or the appearance and passing from one thought, feeling, or mood, to another.

In the midst of an experience that seems especially significant or that presents a particular problem or concern, one can also encounter quite unexpectedly the emptiness within the activity. One may try to mentally unravel the genesis of the situation, pursuing its causes until one's efforts again dissolve into indistinct memories, sensations, and associations, leaving one with only a sense of emptiness or space, with no traceable origin. The spaciousness that permeates thought and activity becomes apparent in moments when one's conceptual framework or usual routine is suddenly shattered. Suddenly one realizes that there is no supporting background protecting or providing one with anything with which to identify. In this little glimpse of unborn spaciousness there is a moment of gratuitous clarity. Like the moment after one has had an accident, one looks up and it is as if the world had come to a stop. All the little details one would not generally notice stand out very clearly and then are swept back into a blur by the onrush of the confusion of pain, thoughts, and feelings.

The momentary recognition of the unborn quality within experience is not a denial of the experience but, in an unexpected way, its essence. The core of activity has nothing to do with conceptualization. The immediacy of experience transcends any effort at conceptualizing it or describing it with words. For conceptualization implies birth and therefore something conditioned, but the actuality of experience is unborn and unconditioned. Pouring water is simply pouring water. One may have had the idea to pour water in order to nourish a plant or prepare tea, but there is nothing conceptual about the act; it just occurs. There is a timeless immediacy to experience that is neither here nor there; the past is fiction and the future a distant dream.

The spaciousness accommodating and permeating experience is the primordial feminine. In referring to space as a primary quality of the feminine, we do not necessarily mean physical space but a space inseparable from the world of one's mind, thoughts, emotions, sensations, perceptions, and bodily activity. This space is simply here, without conditions, either positive or negative. It is open, all pervasive, and without origin.

Describing the feminine as all-accommodating space is not in conflict with its conventional associations, including the capacity for giving birth, nurturing, protecting, and providing warmth and encouragement. Limitless and unconditioned, accommodating all things, this unborn space is the cosmic

6. Mother and child. Mali, 19th century.

8

7. *The Blind Swimmer*, 1934. Max Ernst.

max ernst 1934

8. Supreme Goddess as Void, India, 19th century.

womb in which all contradictions and polarities can coexist; the womb of the feminine neither favors, isolates, not threatens any particular thing. Rather, the fertile space of the feminine is constantly giving birth and is unceasing in its accommodation and penetration of all things. Although it is without beginning or end, the feminine is forever active, providing the open and uncreated ground for the constant revelation and display of the phenomenal world.

Unborn, unceasing, and spacious as the sky, the cosmic feminine womb gives birth to our perception of reality. We experience the rich and colorful world of life and death, of creation and destruction, and of time, space, form, and directions, as qualities of perception. Perceptions themselves are transitory and relative. They come into being and pass away, one after another,

10

and depend upon other perceptions for their meaning and value. All perceptions are thus conditioned and interdependent, having no intrinsic substance. Their origin derives from and dissolves into the unfathomable space of the feminine. Like embryo and womb, our perceptions and their accommodating field are impossible to separate.

Perception occurs through the activities and qualities of touch, taste, smell, sight, hearing, and thought. While it has a seemingly objective point of reference in the external environment, at the same time perception can be described as an internal, mental, and emotional process, subject to individual differentiation. Thus, while the perceiver receives a wide range of stimuli that are focused into perceptions, he or she also has a role in creating and distorting what is perceived.

Perceiver and perceived are actually an inseparable and unique expression of nonduality. Paradoxically, however, this reality is frequently experienced as a dualistic separation between oneself and the world, I and other, exemplified in the distinction one makes between the world of the body and the world of the mind. The analytical, cerebral, or dreamlike imaginings of the mind often appear to be in sharp contrast to the sensory experiences of the body and, by extension, of the entire physical world. However this split is felt or defined, considerable time and energy are then spent trying to line up the apparently disparate elements in order to understand the relationship between them, or to force them to mesh.

9. Joan Miró.

A characteristic feeling associated with duality is doubt, the nagging sense that one can never secure one's identity and territory, or ascertain whether one is completely "together" or not, whether the world outside is all right, or whether one's relationships are stable and secure. Each new event, person, or idea that one encounters can be seen as a potential threat.

One tends to assume that the sense of separation has always existed; one takes it for granted and thus solidifies the sense of division between oneself and the world. The experience of "I" takes on the quality of a castle or fortress with its own moat or self-created defense perimeter. Yet paradoxically, with all this concern for protection, accompanied by feelings of isolation and lone-liness, one is never actually separate. Points of reference, clouded by fears or expectations, become an extension of oneself and are not seen independently or appreciated for what they are.

Duality-creating barriers are of one's own making, but they are often as-sumed to be an integral part of the environment and are difficult to recognize. Barriers are filled with ready-made answers. When an event does not meet or feed one's expectations, or when something does not work out as one had hoped or planned, then there is frequently a pained response: disappoint-ment, resentment, frustration, anger, or fear. These only tend to reinforce the duality previously created.

Occasionally, unexpected exposure to pain can lead to an experience of nonduality. The unexpected removal of the sense of separation and an im-mediate meeting with the world of one's environment momentarily allows one to see things as they are. Stripped of mental baggage, such a sudden encounter is extremely raw, like being plunged into ice water. The customary ways of dividing and sorting out the world are temporarily meaningless and ineffectual.

This momentary destruction of dualistic fixations can bring a terrifying sense of openness, a possibility of actual freedom. The rug has been pulled out from under one's feet, and there is no sense of territory or reference point. The glimpse of nonduality reveals an awesome quality of the feminine: dis-passionate, nonjudgmental, and supporting creation and destruction equally, like the vastness of space without even gravity as a reference point. There is a chilling and primordial sensation that is evoked by this experience of unborn space, yet in its immensity and capacity for containing and nurturing every detail of existence—birth, joy, pain, death—one feels strangely at home. For hidden deep within the all-embracing accommodation of this forebodingly majestic space, one recognizes the inspirational spark that gave birth to the archaic but timeless images of the Great Mother.

In the terrifying openness of unborn space there is a refreshing alertness, a sense that anything might happen. Here is an intelligence, inseparable from limitless space, a primordial insight that sees things in a radically different light. Coexisting with unborn space, this intelligence is distinct from the analytical mind. Initially, it seems contradictory to speak of the feminine, unborn space, as possessing its own intelligence. But this is precisely what is

12

10. Shiva as a corpse having intercourse with the goddess Kali, which symbolizes the terror aroused by the destruction of pre-conceptions.

being said, that there is a self-existing openness within situations that *is* itself a penetrating awareness that appreciates and discriminates the value of each thing.

One of the basic functions of the intelligence of the feminine is to see through dualistic fixations and barriers. This penetrating intelligence can be awakened randomly and unexpectedly. These sudden glimpses of insight into the emptiness existing within activity are often interpreted as frightening and unpleasant events, so that one turns away from them, attempting to cover up or forget about them. One immediate response is often to create another reference point, a dualistic interest or focus to make one feel more secure and comfortable. It seems safer to ignore the existential and experiential dimensions of being; thus one creates a scheme or problem so that one no longer has to face or even remember the encounter with open space.

13

The activity of disregarding and covering up, when compulsively repeated, describes a habitual distortion of space that gives rise to neurotic patterns. No only is one ignoring, but one is also manufacturing a counterfeit reality, filled with methodical planning and elaborate structures and systems. This is generally an unconscious endeavor that seems so normal that there is seldom any reason to question it. Various compartments and pigeonholes are created to accommodate different preconceived situations. Strenuous effort makes the compartments so tight fitting that there is little chance for any gaps or openness to occur. Space, by nature empty and fertile, can become frozen and solid, filled with reference points and programmed with answers.

The process of solidifying space is then an effort to avoid the fertile possibilities of the unborn feminine and its accompanying intelligence. The flashes of awareness and glimpses of unborn space often occur in painful situations; thus one may feel ambiguous about their value. There seems to be something disruptive about cultivating a further sense of clarity and openness; yet there is a seductiveness, a tremendous sense of opportunity and freedom associated with these experiences.

If one allows the spaciousness and the intelligence of the feminine to develop, one may begin to realize the need to relate to confusion more openly, and ironically, to begin to appreciate the value of painful as well as pleasurable experiences. Just as one might have glimpsed the emptiness in experience, so one might now see the intelligence within pain. One begins to realize that acknowledging discomfort and taming one's confusion can give birth to further intelligence and a greater sense of clarity and spaciousness.

In the search for the feminine, the question of origins and ultimate beginnings comes to be seen as inseparable from the effort to understand the nature and quality of both one's own confusion and one's fundamental sanity. The inspiration that led one to penetrate the ever-present matrix of the unborn now points to the existence of an uncompromising and unconditional reality that can only be apprehended through further disciplined efforts to understand oneself and one's own fundamental situation. Uncovering the path of the feminine is an ongoing process inspiring one to see and to relate with things as they are.

11. Fuji Pilgrimage Mandala.

12. Chakrasamvara and his consort Vajravarahi symbolizing the supreme
    joy born of the union of energy and intelligence.

CHAPTER TWO

The Birth of Communication

FEMININE AND MASCULINE portray the basic dynamics of how we function in and relate to the world, as well as the ongoing process of the universe itself. They are not anything in particular outside of oneself, but are inherent characteristics of the mind and of ways of being and acting in the world. The essence of feminine and masculine energy is also a reflection of the dynamics of one's own intelligence and one's capacity for emotional response and communication. The interaction of masculine and feminine is like a precisely orchestrated shadow play, where dark and light, form and emptiness, interpenetrate. Clarity pierces the richness of confusion; despair is present in the midst of joyous celebration.

Born into this world, we cannot escape relationship. The activity of communication, which establishes relationships with the world, is a fundamental characteristic of the masculine. The masculine operates within the vast and empty space of the feminine and is, in fact, provoked by the openness and inviting quality of feminine space. Implicit in this relationship is a quality of passion. The masculine, like the lover courting his beloved, pursues and desires to dissolve into, conquer, and have union with the feminine space. The dispassionate and awesome qualities of the feminine are bewitching, much like the seductive and playful sirens who tormented and captivated Ulysses. They create the impulse in the masculine to respond to the world in a personal and compassionate manner. As the perceiver of the unceasing flow of energy, colors, and textures comprising the animate and inanimate worlds, the masculine encompasses the total range of personal experience: confusion and clarity, pleasure and pain, and the full spectrum of the emotions. The masculine, for all of its changing appearances, is fundamentally indestructible, for it is the essence of everything contained by the unborn.

Associating compassion and personal and emotional expression with the masculine transcends chauvinistic definitions of feminine and masculine. Describing the masculine as an emotional and communicative responsiveness points to the inseparable feminine ground upon which the masculine is dependent. For the masculine is what relates to the unbornness, explores the spaciousness, and articulates the unceasingness of the feminine.

The play of unborn feminine space and unconditional masculine response describes two cosmic principles. The unceasing interpenetration of these principles allows communication and meaningful activity to take place. Although

THE FEMININE the unoriginated space of the feminine gives birth, there is no separation between the vastness of the unborn and its contents, the masculine. Woven into a cloth that is indissoluble, the interplay of feminine and masculine is an expression of the dynamics of creativity. Creative acts, as expressions of the masculine, arise from the feminine ground of creativity, the empty field, uncarved block, or velvety silence that inspires a communicative response.

13. Bear Mother, the primordial genetrix of the Northwest Coast Indians.

14.

Thirty spokes
Share one hub.
Adapt the nothing therein to the purpose at hand, and you can make use of the cart.
Knead clay in order to make a vessel. Adapt the nothing therein to the purpose in
hand, and you can make use of the vessel. Cut out doors and windows in order to
make a room. Adapt the nothing therein to the purpose in hand, and you can make
use of the room.
Thus what we gain is Something, yet it is by virtue of
Nothing that this can be put to use.

Lao Tzu

The spontaneous birth-giving capacity of the feminine bestows a primary motherlike quality upon it. The mother is the container, and her contents, that which is born, is the masculine son. This primordial relationship of mother and son describes a reciprocal relationship that each one of us, regardless of sex, has with the world. At times we may find that the world, whether defined as other people, objects, or natural phenomena, is mothering us; at other moments we may find that we are in a position of mothering the world. As in families, there are undercurrents within this mother and son relationship of mutual resentment, confusion, and envy, as well as expressions of admiration, love, and emulation.

This mythic structure of the mother and son relationship expresses the human need to identify with the cosmic process of creation and destruction. First there is the totality of space, the background that provides immense possibility. Out of this space form arises. The situation becomes activated and dynamic; gases, amino acids, sperm, eggs, and seeds all come into being, and out of this fertile situation birth occurs. The self-fertilization of the world is analogous to a mother who spontaneously produces a child and later becomes its lover. The masculine principle is the form that arises and moves within this space and journeys toward its mother. From primordial times, the feminine as

19

THE FEMININE   the Great Goddess was conceived as mother, lover, and destroyer. The story of Oedipus, who marries his mother, reflects both an incestual taboo as well as the tragedy of literally interpreting the injunction: love thy mother. By contrast, in the Catholic and Greek Orthodox celebration of the Feast of the Assumption, the Virgin Mary is taken to the celestial bridal chamber and rejoined with her son, the King of Kings.

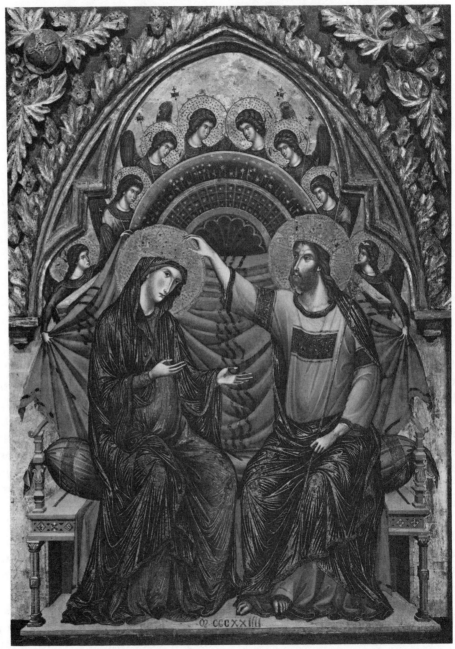

15. *The Coronation of the Virgin*. Paolo Veneziano. 14th century.

The mother and son aspect within each of us has a juiciness and fire that encourages and infuses communication with an emotional and passionate coloring. In the mother and daughter, or father and son, relationship there is a sense of sameness, a known quality, whereas in the mother and son relationship there is a certain unknown quality highlighted by sexual distinction. Although the father and daughter relationship could be spoken of in a similar way, the primariness of the feminine as the mother of all things sets the precedent.

As the unknown, dwelling in a place that one cannot yet see, the mother beckons and calls from afar. The son is that which stirs and strives to encounter and understand the force that is generating the sense of journey and inspiration. Because the son and the mother, the seeker and the unknown, represent a polarity, the masculine in us experiences, as one of the poles, a mixture of pleasure and pain, a desire to know the opposite completely and to totally dissolve into that which is not known. There is an intuitive feeling in the son that once the unrevealed is discovered it will nourish his hunger, quench his thirst, and give solace to his heart as only a mother can.

The danger inherent in the affinity between mother and son resides in its dynamic: a desire for reunion with the unknown, which presupposes a profound sense of separation. Without the quality of the unknown there would be no adventure, whether that of the hero who must conquer dragons and journey over treacherous seas, or that of the spiritual warrior who must master his or her own ignorance and cross the ocean of human suffering. The separation can be seen as an abyss or a perilous voyage with no safeguards or comforting command posts along the way. At times, overwhelmed by hope or fear, the inspiration can develop into an insatiable hunger or preoccupation. Fixating on one's isolation while being obsessed by a desire to experience the unknown creates frustration and problematic situations. Belief in isolation and a desire for union contradict each other so that the spaciousness and beckoning quality of the feminine may be overlooked. One is left with anxiety-filled womblike fantasies—the compulsive urge to immerse oneself, through whatever means, in some kind of behavior that will ultimately guarantee an all-embracing oblivion or self-extinction. Notwithstanding the potential hazards or possible fixations that may occur, the mother and son relationship, as exemplified in the hero's quest or spiritual path, describes a primary quality of journey that each one of us experiences, a path that is sometimes hidden and sometimes clear, leading from bewilderment to knowing.

The unvarying openness and richnness of the feminine also invites the masculine to respond to it as lover. In the play of lover and beloved there is a sense of intrigue and curiosity. Captivated by the color, movement, and forms of the feminine, the masculine lover wishes to explore every part of the beloved. Frequently, the action of the masculine has elements of both son and lover, so that an interwoven pattern of experience develops. When the delight of the lover relationship reaches a peak, the haunting and embracing quality

21

THE FEMININE of the mother is there waiting. The periodic feeling of separation and break in communication between lovers invites a quest for the solace of the mother. In the same way, the sense of distance from the mother provokes a desire and search for the immediacy of the lover.

> *Oh, her beauty—the tender maid! Its brilliance gives light like lamps to one travelling in the dark.*
> *She is a pearl hidden in a shell of hair as black as jet,*
> *A pearl for which Thought dives and remains unceasingly in the deeps of that ocean.*
> *He who looks upon her deems her to be a gazelle of the sand-hills, because of her shapely neck and the loveliness of her gesture.*
>
> Ibn al-'Arabi

16. Prince and Lady prolonging their intercourse. India, 18th century.

What gives vitality and inspiration to any relationship is the intelligence and warmth sparked by communication. Intelligence occurs through opening oneself to the beloved and the mother, by becoming both the lover and the son. At first the pursuit of the feminine can be terrifying, for the intelligence and feelings that are aroused can prove to be threatening. Perhaps one will be rejected, or, becoming more exposed, one might suddenly feel embarrassed by one's nakedness. Most frightening of all is the probability that one will have to totally surrender oneself if one is to make love and know completely the lover and mother.

The challenges of one's choiceless relationship with the feminine require one to develop openness. One could become narcissistic or hedonistic without a sense of sharing or encounter. Making love obsessively to anything at any time, one could become so self-indulgent and aggressive that the lovemaking might turn into masturbation. Perhaps one's frustration or isolation becomes so acute that the attempt to communicate is twisted into a destructive, life-denying force or produces a fear-motivated asceticism. To transcend these clinging fixations, open communication must be developed.

22

Communication implies at least two elements—something perceived as well as a perceiver—and also implied is a commonly shared space accommodating the relationship. Whether from different or similar backgrounds, when two people recognize and feel that they have made real contact with each other, the usual feeling of separateness or alienation falls away, if only for a moment. However the exchange takes place—with words, gestures, or touch—there is a quality of openness, warmth, and intelligence that penetrates the masks of conceptualization that usually pass for communication.

In another situation, one might perceive in an encounter with someone or something that there is an unyielding, antagonistic, or indifferent energy that one should not encourage. In this case communication is the ability to see clearly the quality of energy taking place and to behave appropriately. This is the sense of seeing something in its own perspective, without predetermined barriers, and suggests a fundamentally noncentralized space in which everything is interrelated and accommodated by the ever-present atmosphere of the unborn feminine. Because the unborn both contains and is inseparable from whatever is experienced and perceived, it can also be communicated and expressed through symbols.

17.   Male and female figures. Luba, Congo, 19th century.

As gestures, signs, or acts, symbols are a direct communication of reality, revealing and expressing the highlights of experience. Without symbols communication is barren and lifeless, going nowhere, without a path or a journey. In the noncentralized space where communication occurs, the union of perceiver and perceived spontaneously gives birth to symbols. The primordially unceasing interrelatedness of the world and the mind is articulated through symbols manifest in infinite forms and patterns of energy.

The common understanding of a symbol is that it stands for something greater than itself. When symbols are defined in this manner, the vividness of things is obscured, and one's mental attitude is dulled by the blinders of conventional associations. In this condition symbols take on an inert, standardized meaning, and communication is robbed of its juiciness.

Cut off from the immediacy of experience and dwelling in the bleak world of dualistic isolation, one imagines, hopes, and believes that there might be another or better world separate from this one—whether it is thought of as some kind of afterlife, utopian future, or idealized past. Interpreted or used to reinforce a dualistic point of view, symbols are manipulated to raise hope, to soothe or promote fears, or to solidify a particular kind of identity.

The distinction between looking and seeing throws light on the difference between the dual and nondual approach to symbols. By *looking* we mean the effort to project expectations onto the environment. Even before seeing anything, one may be searching for validation, or hunting out those qualities that could destroy or negate one's goals. This process of using symbolism to conceptualize or strategize blinds one to what is actually presenting itself. Accustomed as we are to looking, the world appears to us to be very flat; its depths, highlights, and subtleties are hidden by projections and conceptualizations about experience. Viewing the world in this way brings a sense of double identity: what one would like to see might be there, but there might be also something else present, lurking behind the facade of our projections.

Seeing involves an attitude of acceptance and unbiased appreciation of reality. To see in this way involves the development of a way of being that depends on ongoing discipline. This discipline encourages and provides a space for one to face up to one's blindspots and to surrender the expectations that block the ability to see. The discipline of seeing is an ongoing process of learning how to live and work with the world as it is, while knowing that one is completely inseparable from it. With the field of experience unobstructed by projections and conceptualizations, whatever one sees has vibrancy and depth. When one learns to see, there is no loss of energy in trying to maintain a particular view of the world, and one can develop a receptivity that need not cling to any specific frame of reference. If one no longer feels alienated from experience, there is a genuine appreciation for all the details and aspects of one's world.

Seeing provides a nondual basis of communication in which the awakened masculine responds to the self-existing feminine. The most primary and universal symbols establish an orientation and grounding within the all-

18. *Black Abstraction*. 1927. Georgia O'Keeffe.

embracing space of the feminine. They are part of the act of seeing, and in this sense, as a direct communication of reality, they are the most immediate expression of the basic qualities of experience. Symbols do not represent anything other than what is. They express the question of and the quest for life's meaning that ultimately leads to statements about how we were born, how the universe evolved, and how the inspiration of the genesis of things is continually operating within us. In evoking cosmological processes, symbols fulfill the need to articulate for oneself an understanding of how one's reality came into being.

In the *tai chi* symbol the matrix of the unborn feminine is described by the circle encompassing the primal interplay of masculine and feminine energies. The sinuous division between the light *yang* and the dark *yin* initially arises from the masculine responding to the provocative spaciousness and intelligence of the unborn feminine ground. In a condition of mutual and perpetual transformation, the unceasing interplay of *yin* and *yang*, feminine and masculine, dark and light, comprises the relative world—the world of appearances, impermanence, and unending phenomenal change. This relative world of activity is made transparent, thoroughly penetrated by and inseparable from the absolutely spacious unborn feminine.

The sustaining power of the feminine, like the sky, expands into the seemingly immeasurable distances of outer space. The activity of the masculine, responding and wanting to explore and probe the vast unchartered realms of space, is highlighted in the situation of the astronaut. Hurtling through the velvety darkness of space, the astronaut is part of an elaborate and sophisticated network of communication. Although there is something heroic about the astronaut, he or she is completely dependent upon a vast system monitoring the life functions and controlling the spacecraft. The astronaut's role is defined and inspired by the reality of the feminine, represented by the enveloping, dark mantle of space accommodating with sublime indifference the galaxies, spaceship, and astronaut. The feminine further defines the situation insofar as the astronaut must develop a receptiveness and submissiveness to be able to act and communicate.

Encapsulated by precision-tooled protective wear and an intricate electronic environment, the astronaut is like an embryo. The whole exploratory process and technology that make the journey possible are like a placenta that nourishes and supports the astronaut. The womb as well as the consort of the astronaut is space itself. Liberated from gravitational fields, he or she can float freely in space open to the immensity of an experience without reference point.

The image of the astronaut and his or her precarious relation to the unknown reaches of space is a provocative statement about the nature of intelligence. Like the astronaut's training and work, the discipline of awakening insight involves the development of an ever more precise skill in communicating. The continuing process of developing intelligence is the heart of communication, the awakened interplay of feminine and masculine.

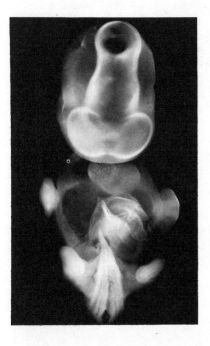

19. Six-week human embryo.

20.

21.

CHAPTER THREE

Symbols Without Origin

LIKE A DIAMOND so sharp it might cut itself, the symbols of developing intelligence emerge with pristine clarity from the rich and spacious matrix of the unborn. In appreciating the feminine and working with its subtle nuances, one is also exploring the nature of mind, for the essence of mind is space; thoughts, feelings, and perceptions may appear, disappear, and reappear, but there is no place for anything to rest or become permanently established. This emptiness, openness, or void, is the feminine aspect of mind. Similarly the body which seems so solid, is in continual flux and is just as nonsubstantial as the mind.

> *The body, like a hollow bamboo, has no substance,*
> *Mind is like the essence of space, having no place for thoughts.*
> *Rest loose your mind; neither hold it nor permit it to wander.*
> *If mind has no aim, it is mahamudra.*
> *Accomplishing this is the attainment of supreme enlightenment.*
>
> Tilopa

The open quality of the feminine generates basic intelligence. Like space, intelligence has no final measurement and can be located nowhere and everywhere. Although fundamentally a feminine aspect of mind, intelligence is activated by the responsive clarity of the masculine. As an ability to communicate and relate skillfully, action has a masculine quality, inseparable from the space of the feminine. The unborn feminine is the ground from which any kind of appropriate activity of the masculine grows.

The fertile ground of the feminine is like the cervix, the gateway through which all human life emerges. The passageway of mortality, the cervix is a primordial symbol announcing the human drama of birth and death. While in the womb, the embryo's head is protected by the two crescent-shaped cervical lips. At the time of birth the embryo pushes downward, and the pressure on the cervical lips increases until the cervix finally opens, allowing and facilitating the fetus' emergence from the dark water-world to the world of air and brightness.

The structure of the cervix evokes images of horns, whose shapes are primordially associated with the crescent moon.* As personifications of the

---

*The word cervix is derived from an Indo-European root, *ker-*, which means horn or head, with derivatives referring to horned animals, or horn-shaped objects.

22. The goddess Isis. Egypt, 8th-6th century B.C.

23. Carved and painted wood. Australian Aborigine.

fertility and inspiring intelligence of the feminine ground, Great Mother goddesses—such as Isis, the Virgin Mary, or White Buffalo Cow Woman—wear, are embellished with, or are seated upon the horns of the crescent moon. They preside over the birth and development of cosmic insight and the attainment of wisdom.

Passing through the gate of horns, the newborn is ushered into another realm of being. As it first emerges from the womb the head is momentarily embraced by the cervical horns. The crown of horns (or traditionally any crown) is a universal symbol of confirmation, celebrating passage from one condition of being and awareness to another.

30

It is an immemorial intuition that the mystery of birth and death are inseparable, if not identical. The source of birth and death, the place we came from and to which we are going, is archetypically the same space.

You're so beautiful, you gotta die someday.

Blues refrain

Thus, the cervix of the feminine unborn, which is continually begetting human life and everything we know and do not know, is equally the whirlpool of creation and destruction, whose unceasing motion nothing can resist. In its impartiality it is like a vast charnel ground, barren and desolate, receiving without question the bodies of the dead. The image of a charnel ground is of a place where corpses are dumped without any regard for burial and are left exposed to the elements to decompose, providing food for vultures, ravens, jackals, and other beasts of prey. As the matrix and receptacle of death and impermanence, the charnel ground is a primal symbol of the destruction of illusion, expressing a state in which the mind is stripped of all its conceptual adornments so that one's naked intelligence encounters the mother space of the unborn. The depiction of ravaging and devouring mother

24. Terrible Goddess Kali. India.

31

25. Demon Dance. Bali.

goddesses personifies this aspect of the unborn, mercilessly and impersonally destroying that to which it has given birth. The East Indian Rangda, with her drooling tongue, scooping up innocent children; or the Aztec Coatlicue with her serpent skirt, breastplate of hands, and fiercely hungry double-headed serpent head, exemplify the terrifying and inevitable majesty of death and the fear of having one's comfortable cloak of ignorance destroyed.

The reality of birth and death implies continual change: growth and decay, rising and falling. This motion of the world could seem random and meaningless were it not for the hints of a larger meaning or order, presented to us by phenomena such as the waxing and waning of the moon or the turning of the seasons.

The swastika is a fundamental symbol reflecting the unceasing flow of phenomenal change. It portrays the generative feminine as a totality of motion and energy. Like the continual emergence of conditioned being from the cervix of the unborn, the swastika also is generated from a central point which in this case extends uniformly in the four cardinal directions. The motion of time and the continuous activity and energy that characterize phenomenal existence cause the four arms of the swastika to bend. Underlying the objective observation that the swastika describes solar movement and the progression of the seasons is the intuition that the inevitability of cyclical movement in the cosmos bears upon one's own personal journey.

26. Coatlicue, Goddess of the Serpent Skirt. Aztec, 15th century.

The structure of the swastika describes a process to which all conditioned phenomena, including the universe itself, are subject: formation, stasis, destruction, and extinction. The word universe—one turn—defines itself as a circular movement that naturally completes itself by going through the four phases of growth and decay. As a finite manifestation of limitless space, the entire universe expresses the nature of the endlessly procreative feminine.

The processes that govern the universe may be comprehended as analogous to those operating within a single human life; this has aroused in us the motivation to know and experience the fullness and extent of the phenomenal world directly through our own being. Identifying one's existence with the inevitable order that characterizes existence can produce a sense of deeply rooted well-being. The original Sanskrit meaning of swastika is precisely that—well-being.

27.

28.

29.

Despite present-day associations with the Nazi party and World War II, the swastika's appearance as a life-affirming symbol spans both hemispheres. Throughout North and South America the swastika is incised, woven, or painted on ceremonial vessels, pottery, baskets, ritual clothing, and ornaments; it also is a major unifying motif in emergence myths, cosmic histories, and accounts of spiritual journeys. In Eurasia the swastika enhances the representations of the goddesses who preside over fertility, life, and the multitudinous forms of nature, often adorning their hands, breasts, wombs, and clothing. With its intrinsic meaning of unending motion and all-encompassing activity, throughout Europe and Asia the swastika has been etched on spindle whorls, painted on palace walls, incised in caves, and woven into the garments of royalty and peasant alike.

Highlighting the understanding of the flow of impermanence ceaselessly generated from the unborn, the swastika is also a vital symbol in the stories of the Buddha and in related Buddhist teachings and practices handed down to the present. When Prince Siddhartha, the historical Buddha, became fully determined to understand the nature of impermanence and suffering, he set off for the Bodhi tree. Just before reaching the tree, to the right side of the road, Siddhartha saw a tuft of swastika grass.* The king of the Nagas, a powerful water-dwelling serpent spirit, presented the grass to the prince. Taking the grass, Siddhartha walked around the Bodhi tree three times and then spread it around the tree with the tops of the grass pointing inward and the roots outward. He then sat beneath the tree facing east and, concentrating his mind, said:

> May, as long as I sit here, my body wither away,
> May the skin, the bones and the flesh decay,
> But until I have attained Enlightenment
> Which is hard to be secured even during many aeons,
> I shall not move from this spot.
>
> *Lalitavistara*

This ritual incident preceding the enlightenment of the Buddha expresses the relationship between the understanding of the unending motion of existence and the realization of an awakened and indestructible intelligence. The use of the swastika as a symbol of enlightenment derives from the sense of indestructible well-being arising from accepting the nature of the world and seeing things as they are.

After the death of the Buddha, the *Parinirvana*, and prior to the development of an actual iconographic image of the Buddha some five centuries later, the swastika, along with the Dharmachakra (the Wheel of the Law), was one of the main symbols of the awakened state of the Buddha. The swastika is often found on images of the Buddha's footprint, indicating its significance as an integral aspect of the path of developing intelligence and skillful behavior.

30. Buddha's footprint.

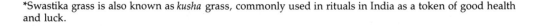

*Swastika grass is also known as *kusha* grass, commonly used in rituals in India as a token of good health and luck.

34

Although the swastika has continued to be used in the Buddhist art of Japan, China, and Tibet, its innermost meaning has also been communicated through the verbal teachings of Buddhism. The Buddha taught that to see things clearly, as they are, requires an acknowledgment of the reality of suffering, sickness, old age, and death. These facts of life point to the inescapable truth of impermanence, epitomized in the relentless motion of the swastika.

31.

The emphasis in Buddhism on accepting the painful facts of life is designed to enable man and woman to see and work with the intelligence that is inseparable from the vast space of the feminine. The recognition of the transitory nature of all things can lead one to experience the fundamental all-pervasive emptiness that underlies the world of endless change. This emptiness is indistinguishable from the open space of the cervix of the unborn.

In the beginning nothing comes.
In the middle nothing stays.
In the end nothing goes.

Milarepa

The realization of emptiness is an aspect of a journey based on bridging or eliminating the sense of separation that exists between I and other, lover and beloved, and son and mother. As long as there is a journey, there is a growth characterized by ever more skillful seeing, relating, and communicating with the world.

35

32. The sea-mother's coral tree of life.

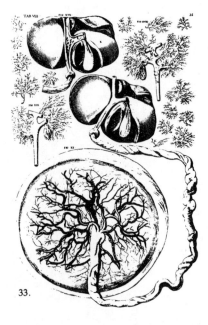

33.

A symbol of this journey is the tree of life. Closely related to the swastika, it is associated with the power of continuous regeneration. As a motif occurring in the creation myths of the Near East, Europe, and the Americas, the tree of life bursts forth from the earth, the cervix of the unborn, bringing with it earth's amniotic waters. With the umbilical cord and foetal membranes forming its structure, the tree of life spirals skywards, bearing all living forms on its branches. Its spinning movement gives rise to the four winds and four rivers of life. The Cunas of San Blas, Panama, say that the whirlpool created by the turning of the tree is the vulva of the Earth Mother, the center from which all is born and to which all returns.

As a cosmic axis, the tree of life is the center of a mandala, a circle of all-accommodating space with no corners in which to hide and where everything is exposed. Being a primary expression of the unborn, the mandala is

36

the groundless ground, an utter openness embracing the entire spectrum of experience. Its contents reflect the rich diversity of the patterns of energy comprising the universe as the interplay and union of perceiver and perceived.

In the European alchemical tradition the tree as the cosmic axis is associated with the tree of knowledge. The understanding of universal law is grounded in an inevitably evolving core—the tree of wisdom—from which all understanding and laws emanate. According to the Rosicrucians, this tree is rooted in the unfathomable depths of the sky while its branches flower and spread through the fertile and shifting movements of the earth.

In the story of the Buddha, the tree of life is the Bodhi tree, which is also the tree of enlightenment. Seated beneath the tree, the Buddha remained unswayed by the seductions of the daughters of Mara, or illusion—the projections of Buddha's own doubts and fantasies. Called upon by Mara to bring forth a witness to his enlightenment, the Buddha replied: "The earth is my witness!" Striking the earth with his right hand, Buddha continued:

> This earth is the support of all the living beings;
> It is equal and impartial
> With regard to all that does and does not move.
> May it bear evidence that I do not lie,
> And may it be the witness before you.

As Buddha said this the earth shook six times, and out came Sthavara, the goddess of the earth. With folded hands she spoke:

> O Highest of beings, so it is. As you have said, so it is perfectly true. It is all evident and clear to me. But, O Lord, you yourself are the highest witness of the truth for all the world including the gods.

Finishing her speech the earth goddess disappeared, leaving the Buddha seated alone beneath the tree of life and enlightenment, where, withstanding a final assault of doubt and temptation, he soon attained supreme enlightenment.

For seven weeks after attaining enlightenment, the Bodhi tree was the Buddha's point of reference. The foot of the tree where he sat was the *bodhimanda*, the center of the mandala of enlightenment. The first week he remained immovable in a cross-legged posture and contemplated the tree. The second week he journeyed through numberless metaphysical and cosmological world systems. The third week he again contemplated the Bodhi tree without shutting his eyes. Following various travels to different parts and levels of the world, in the seventh week the Buddha again sat beneath the Bodhi tree. There a group of traveling merchants encountered him, and he finally left the tree with a begging bowl and began the journey that, for the next forty-five years until his death, was spent articulating the teaching that he realized while seated at the foot of the tree.

The roots of the tree of life are lost in the realm of the feminine unborn. The cervix of the unborn is the place where the tree emerges from the earth,

34. Female tree spirit, from the stupa at Sanchi, India.

37

35. Tree of Death. German, 16th century.

marking the spot where the Buddha attained supreme wisdom. This place is also referred to as the *vajra asana*, the seat of indestructibility. The association of the moment of awakening and wisdom with so earthy a place as the foot of a tree points to the simple and uncompounded nature of enlightenment.

According to orthodox Christian tradition, the tree of knowledge was given by God to Adam and Eve in the Garden of Eden with the admonition that eating its fruit would lead to the fall from immortality. Temptation, in the form of a serpent, seduced Eve into picking a fruit. After taking a bite, she in turn seduced Adam to share of the fruit, and this led to their expulsion from the Garden. Adam and Eve's primordial transgression is what inspired God to send Christ to earth in order to redeem humankind. Christ achieved collective redemption by being crucified on the cross, symbolizing the tree of life and knowledge. The cross is a continual reminder of the possibility for purification and the attainment of an awakened condition of life.

38

36. *Crucifixion.* Albrecht Dürer.

Recent scholarship has discovered other variations of the Genesis story of the Garden of Eden that were current in the first few centuries after the crucifixion and prior to the establishment of Church orthodoxy. In one story the serpent tells Eve that by eating the fruit of the tree of knowledge she and Adam will become godlike, knowing the difference between good and evil. After they had eaten, "the light of knowledge shone upon them," and indeed they became as gods. In this version the serpent is the servant of the Highest God, "the All," and bears resemblance to the Naga king who offered Buddha the swastika grass. Adam and Eve were expelled from the Garden by an inferior class of gods, the Archons, who were blinded by envy.

In dying on the tree of life, Christ redeemed the wisdom Adam and Eve lost when they left the Garden, and asked others to follow his example by carrying their own crosses. Feeling the weight and responsibility of one's own cross symbolizes here the acceptance of one's total life situation, including

39

suffering and isolation. Thereby a return to the tree of life—to knowledge and ultimate origins—can be achieved.

Opening to pain and confusion is the heart of the journey of developing intelligence. On this path, one may attempt to trace the origins of one's life and suffering, in the hope that if one could find where the journey began, one could experience again the blissful or pure state that preceded pain. Through this unraveling there may be glimpses of the unborn, hints that there is no exact point of origin other than one's own birth, and even that has its own mysteries.

At the same time that one is retracing one's path, a practical motivation to make sense of everyday experience also presents itself. There is a need to live in harmony with one's mundane world and to relate as clearly as possible to the ongoing flow of events. Yet, while trying to live as simply and directly as possible, there is always the possibility that the apple cart might be upset. In the midst of the apples tumbling all over, the disorientation and irritation of the unexpected can give birth to a momentary glimpse of intelligence and space. Spontaneously occurring amidst confusion and unknowing, this little flash is the timeless beginning of the journey that is without end.

The primordial awakening of intelligence is told in the Winnebago story of the primal cultural hero, Hare. Having created the world, Earth Maker realized that his last creation, human beings, were also his most vulnerable progeny. In order to aid and protect humans from destruction by malevolent spirits, he sent forth four protectors. They each became involved in their own selfishness and were unable to perform their duty, so that a fifth protector, Hare, had to be sent out.

Filled with tremendous compassion for human beings, his aunts and uncles, with whom he identified in every way, he incarnated in a woman's womb and attained virgin birth. Hare then traveled across the earth, battling and destroying all the evil spirits. Having achieved his heroic mission, he returned to a sacred lodge and spoke with his grandmother, the spirit of the earth. Proudly he told her that now all of his aunts and uncles were to be immortal like himself. His grandmother replied, "How can that be? Everything in the world and about the world is destined for death and decay." Hare pleaded with her that all humans might be immortal. She answered, "If that is what you want then follow me as I walk the road of life around the world. But don't look back!"

Treading after her, Hare paused and could not resist turning around and looking back. No sooner did he glance back at the place where their journey had begun than the whole site instantaneously collapsed. "O grandson, o grandson, what have you done? I thought you were a man, a person of real prominence. But now you have done it! In no way can decay and death be taken back from your aunts and uncles, the humans." At this point Hare was beside himself with grief, and his mind was assailed by the thought: "To all things death will come!" Wherever he looked, skies, trees, cliffs, and rivers dissolved in front of him. Whatever he directed his mind to, collapsed and was destroyed.

37. Ancient Hopi pottery design symbolizing the universal journey of human understanding.

40

His grandmother and Earth Maker realized that Hare had to develop greater maturity about the ways of the world and that he needed a deeper sense of compassion in order to accept the order of life. Earth Maker said to Hare that rather than despairing, he could relate with warmth and friendliness toward his human aunts and uncles by presenting them with a sacred teaching. Hare finally understood the wisdom of this counsel and brought to the Winnebago the Medicine Rite, the tradition that demonstrated the continuity of the road of life and the road of death. In this way Hare developed intelligence and communication out of his own painful realizations.

Although the journey of developing intelligence has a birth, its roots are without origin, extending into the realm of the unborn—the mother of all intelligence. Born from beginningless space and having no end, the journey can be described as a labyrinth, a spiral tracing of the cosmological quest. Whether it is depicted by the ground plan of a temple, as markings on the earth, or as a painted diagram, the labyrinth represents the journey within the world of the mind. As a play of form and space, the labyrinth makes transparent the all-encompassing and all-pervasive matrix of the unborn.

The drama of the labyrinth is the tension between the forms of one's conditioned thoughts and feelings and the intelligence of the unborn manifest as the space in which the actual journey takes place. Paradoxically, without the structures of thoughts, emotions, and expectations, there would be no journey. The labyrinth is simultaneously a map of neurotic mind and awakening intelligence.

The one who walks the labyrinthine path is the seeker, the masculine son returning to his mother. The mother is the all-accommodating space of the unborn, the matrix allowing the labyrinth of the phenomenal world to come into being. It is this son in us who, by being receptive to the original, unceasing quality of the feminine, is capable of unraveling doubt and knowing the true nature of mind.

38.

39.

CHAPTER FOUR

The Labyrinth of Knowing

In the middle of the journey of our life
I came to myself in a dark wood where
the straight way was lost.

Dante, *Divine Comedy, Canto I*

AS THE WORLD IS ceaselessly changing, coming into being and passing away, we too are constantly moving through the space of life. Although we may sometimes feel that we are standing still, in actuality we are continually involved in a journey. Even when we say about our lives that "things are running smoothly," a sense of journey is implied. While our affairs are on an even keel we rarely question if there is a journey; or, if there is, what its nature might be. We are just someplace in the middle of things, taking care of business. Although the path may seem to roll easily beneath our feet, by relaxing too much we may miss a quick turn and fall on our face.

Tripped up and caught on the sharp edge of a circumstance one asks: where did this journey begin and where will it lead? Or, one may suddenly feel walled in, enveloped in a cloak of claustrophobia in which the space becomes impenetrable and one feels totally isolated. Life's journey reveals a labyrinthine quality. It may seem that one is going nowhere, has come from nowhere, and may have no destiny or purpose at all.

The labyrinthine quality may come to one during the height of pleasure or success, as a feeling of being haunted, a sense of loneliness, or a foreboding of the fleeting nature of the delight. The present enjoyment seems so vulnerable. Pleasure may be quickly replaced by a longing for something more or better—an even larger business venture, a yet more stunning and provocative painting to be created. One can also experience unexpected disappointment accompanying the thrill of success. The pleasure drifts in and out of awareness, creating the feeling of a maze.

Conflicting emotions of pleasure and pain, joy and apathy, arise frequently in life and evoke both bewilderment and intelligence. The awareness of one's confusion seems to have a life of its own. In its brief light one catches a glimpse of the complex and sometimes puzzling quality of one's life and sees the contrasting features of the world in stark and multifaceted juxtaposition. One does not know whether one's life is progressing or going backwards. The choices are equally suggestive and risky.

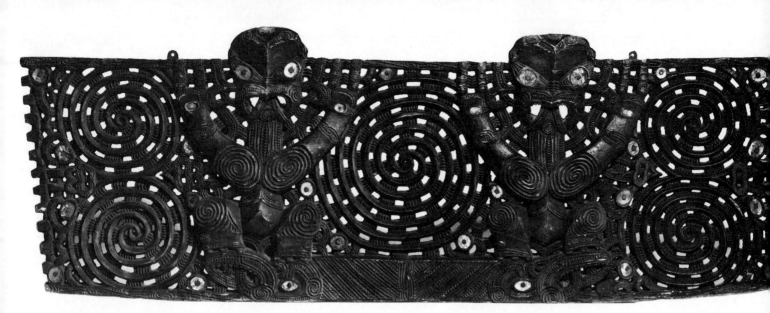

40. Carved Maori labyrinth with spirit figures.

Once one recognizes this labyrinthine, hide-and-seek quality in life, a natural inclination may be to seek the source of confusion, where one might have gone wrong or have made a foolish decision. A tantalizing question arises: if one could find the point where confusion begins, could there then be a way of emerging? How could one find or accomplish it? No matter how many passageways one discovers during the unraveling, there may be nothing that corresponds to the goal or heart of the matter. All the struggle and effort involved in trying to penetrate one's resistances and doubts leaves one trapped in the maze, still living amidst corridors and paths, doors opening and closing.

Yet in the midst of one's search, feeling confused and claustrophobic, one may suddenly find room to breathe, space to move in, and turn around and see what is happening. Resentment or embarrassment may vanish for an instant. The experience of this primordial perceptive intelligence is momentary, and like the labyrinthine play of solidity and emptiness, it is difficult and tricky to pursue or regain. One momentarily spots a face in a crowd and then loses all trace of it; yet the memory of the face lingers and haunts one.

This glimpse of insight is a spark of light that reveals a greater expanse of space than one had thought originally existed. One finds oneself in the accommodating environment of the unborn feminine and discovers that the critical intelligence that resides there is no different than the space that permeates one's being and acting in the world. The aspiration to follow this primordial intelligence, though difficult to realize, is the thread or path that unravels the mystery of the labyrinth.

In the classic story of the slaying of the minotaur, Theseus is able to pass through the labyrinth because his lover, Ariadne, the priestess of the moon, gives him a magical ball of thread. Inspired by Ariadne, the embodiment of wisdom, and guided by her thread, Theseus can penetrate the puzzling interplay of the labyrinth's solidity and emptiness. Finally reaching the center of the labyrinth, he encounters the minotaur, part man and part bull, the half-

41. Prehistoric pottery design representing the endless motion of life and death.

44

brother of the priestess of wisdom. By conquering the minotaur, Theseus pierces the hybrid monster of confused mind. He slays his own confusion and recognizes the play of bewilderment and intelligence. Emerging from the labyrinth and fully embracing Ariadne, Theseus acquires the wisdom and the strength to rule Knossos and continue his life's journey.

Theseus' conquest of the minotaur and consequent emergence from the labyrinth describe an initiation into wisdom. Initiation is an opening and a surrendering to the all-embracing space and intelligence of the feminine. Exertion is called for on the part of the initiate; he or she is not just passively receiving essential teachings or fundamental knowledge. To embrace the primordial intelligence of the unborn, one surrenders one's fears and owns up to one's weaknesses. Without an emptying, there would be no meeting with intelligence. The process of initiation tests the ability to surrender. The abstract decision to open is not quite enough. One does not know what one's capacities are until faced with a situation. There may be a blind spot, a tiny corner that one does not notice or want to reveal. One may want to keep some little hope, desire, or pleasure separate and safe. Initiation does not necessarily end with the hero or heroine blissfully walking off into the sunset. Having received the first initiation, a long and perilous road to full maturity still lies ahead.

42.

The seductive qualities of the experience of vast space and penetrating insight can also provoke anxiety. No one enjoys having one's foolishness, arrogance, or pride exposed. Even when one becomes aware of one's shortcomings, one still lives in a situation that requires immediate attention. In the process of initiation and surrender one is literally hanging by a thread, the thread of critical intelligence connecting one to both clarity and confusion. When one is searching for wisdom, the imperative to act becomes a test. Yet there is no one giving the test who has all the right answers, nor is there necessarily any book of rules that contains the correct solutions. What is being tested is the ability to respond skillfully, with clarity and a sense of the larger environment in which one's actions occur.

43. Mahāvidyā Cinnamastā, the seduction and destruction of illusion. India, 18th century.

During his circuitous journey home following the Trojan War, Ulysses comes upon Aeaea, the death isle of the bewitching and celebrated magician, Circe. Daughter of the sun and an ocean nymph, Circe represents the trickster whose sorcery we experience as the unceasing shiftiness of our perceptions. In her keen-witted capacity to play with the bewildering tendencies of the mind, Circe turned Ulysses' men into pigs. Through his cunning, Ulysses persuaded her to change the pigs back into men, and to allow him and his crew to return home. Yet Circe's seductions were so enchanting and convincing that Ulysses forgot the purpose of his voyage and remained with her for over a year. Finally he heeded his men's reminders and reproaches to set sail for home.

Circe granted Ulysses' desire under the condition that the path home first lead to the land of the dead, the Halls of Hades, where he must consult the blind and androgynous prophet Tiresias for further knowledge of his destiny. In the middle of Ulysses' great fear and depression at the thought of going to the land of the dead and attempting to return, Circe gave him encouragement, inspiration, and guidance.

46

Ulysses acquired strength and wisdom through this test. His ignorance was confronted, and he had to symbolically die to himself by entering the Hall of Hades. To die to oneself is to meet and fully experience one's worst fears, the epitome of which is the fear of death itself. The terror of death is a last gasp, a final effort at preserving one's territory. It is the mortal dread that the boundary that separates one's own private space will dissolve into the unfamiliar and unexpected. What is the ultimate boundary? Is it the fear of losing one's own body? Or is it the fear that oneself and one's achievements will not be remembered; that like a candle flame, one will simply be snuffed out? Is not our ultimate fear the fear of the unknown?

Seduced, frightened, and inspired by Circe's ability to play with his bewilderment and intelligence, Ulysses, in being sent to Hades, was initiated into the unknown. The intensity of his fear and confusion built up to an explosive point whereupon he finally opened to Circe's insight and guidance. Submitting to a seemingly hopeless situation and surrendering his desire for self-preservation, Ulysses' courage to meet the unknown was born.

Ulysses' boldness derived from his acceptance of his fundamental aloneness. Desolate of amusement and diversion, a spark of intelligence occurred that burned away the hope that someone or some greater force outside of himself would provide some kind of salvation. Immersion in the space of aloneness provided the realization of a heroic way, the path that can only be traveled by oneself. Being alone is not like being a little speck in a vacuum or a prisoner in solitary confinement. To acknowledge aloneness is to acknowledge the fullness of being and acting in the world, with wisdom and without hesitation. No matter where one is, what one is doing, or with whom, one is alone. Recognizing aloneness is then the capacity for developing skillful and compassionate relationships with the infinite aspects of the intelligence and the space in which one lives.

44.

45. "Reclining upon a bed was a princess of radiant beauty." Gustave Doré.

The labyrinthine path one is walking is created and articulated by the relationships one develops with space. Because one is fundamentally alone, space becomes one's partner. Tricky, elusive, yet promising growth and richness, space becomes the seeker's bride. In this cosmic drama that occurs within each of us, the feminine challenges and invites the masculine to be heroic and compassionate. Inseparable, feminine and masculine are expressions of the same indestructible reality. Skillful and compassionate masculine behavior is born from opening to the spaciousness and intelligence of the feminine. The space of the feminine requires the capable activity of the masculine in order to be articulated, and feminine intelligence also needs the discipline of the masculine to be actualized.

Given the slipperiness of perceptions and the speed with which situations follow each other, one's daily experiences occur essentially in the midst of a labyrinth that contains both confusion and intelligence. Though one has glimpses of clarity and openness, the play between enlightened and confused behavior seems erratic, self-perpetuating and with no apparent order. Seduced into anticipation of further awareness or pleasure, one may desire to make sense of the seeming chaos of the journey and to penetrate more intimately the quality of space and intelligence that permeates the labyrinthine path.

One may want to explore all aspects of the clarity that seems to underly experience, as a lover wishes to merge with the beloved, to caress, taste, smell, listen, and unite with the loved one forever. The attraction and yearning for the intelligence and spaciousness that wisdom provides is expressed in the passionate relationship between lovers. Thirsting to hold onto the moment of pleasure, one tries to prolong the immersion in and ecstasy of union. Suddenly the intensity of the encounter is over, leaving but the trace of a memory. One is left, the bewildered prince in the fairy tale, holding Cinderella's glass slipper. Haunted by a reminder that one's lover is out there, some-

48   46. *Knight's Dream.* Moritz von Schwind.

THE FEMININE where, one wishes to discover a way in which one can reencounter the inspiring freshness of primordial intelligence. So intense is the desire for union and companionship that one is willing to divest oneself of distracting props, indulgences, and economic, social, or spiritual pretenses.

At the moment of orgasm each partner may experience a dissolving, a drowning or sense of self-extinction. The calling, beckoning quality that draws one on during sexual union is the voice of the feminine, challenging one to open to its spaciousness and respond with complete compassion and warmth. In its indescribability and sense of release, orgasm is like other breakthroughs or encounters with the nonconceptual space of the unborn feminine.

However intense, ecstatic experience is disappointingly momentary. One soon looks forward to the next opportunity for such pleasure or fantasizes multiple orgasms or climax without end. A similar passion inspires our journey into the vastness of psychological space, toward the unceasing intelligence of the feminine. Since sexual climax affords an opportunity to enter into nondual space, this aspiration for a complete and joyous dissolving is like the yearning for wisdom. In aspiring toward wisdom one craves the experience of union with an all-embracing, nurturing, and unceasingly fertile lover and motherlike energy. This longing for the feminine is not necessarily a nostalgia for, or a regression into, childhood, nor need it be an abdication of responsibility. Rather this yearning can lead, paradoxically, to a greater realization of the

47.

space of one's aloneness. Because one has surrendered to the beloved and has allowed oneself to be stripped naked, the experience of the transitoriness of ecstasy puts one directly in touch with the painful unsatisfactoriness of things. At the same time, one gains insight into the essential emptiness and openness underlying experience.

The universal and provocative symbolism of the son making love to the mother, who then becomes the lover, is coupled with the need to kill the father. If the son is the seeker attempting to make his way back to the mother to experience the primal nakedness of mind and the purity and simplicity of being, then the father is the accumulation of confusion and agression that must be killed and transmuted into the enlightened energy of the hero himself. The mother and the father lie within oneself. There is no loving of the mother without the killing of the father. If the confused energy of the father is destroyed, then one can fully and freely make love to the mother; in this union she too is dissolved. What remains is the singular taste of wisdom.

Wisdom, like the intelligence described earlier, has a profoundly feminine nature. It has been universally associated with timelessness, which, like the unborn, precedes birth and endures after the last star has been extinguished. As an expression of the unceasingness of the feminine, wisdom sparks the spontaneous ability to act intelligently without preconceptions. Like space, wisdom is empty of intrinsic content, is all-pervading and continually occurring.

When a person's action is described as a "wise move" or a "wise decision," we usually mean that the person was so attuned to the entire situation that he or she was right on the spot and acted appropriately. Wisdom is also epitomized in common sense. To be actualized, however, the feminine quality of wisdom needs the skill and spontaneity of the masculine. A truly wise approach to everyday life cannot be planned or strategized like a series of formulas or prescriptions. We find an example of this in the well-known story of King Solomon and his difficult task of determining the true mother of a child. The wisdom of the situation could not have been expressed had it not been for the dilemma presented to Solomon. His decision to cut the child in two and give one half to each of the women sparked intelligence and compassion in the rightful mother. She begged that the child be yielded to the pretender, thus exposing the false mother who remained indifferent to the child's fate. Wisdom exists independent of our attempts to attain or ignore it, yet man and woman have been drawn to its power since time began. It is inseparable from and of the same nature as mind; like space and mind, wisdom describes the nonconceptual reality of the feminine.

In various societies wisdom has been personified as a goddess or a spiritually inspired woman. As Dante's Beatrice, or Goethe's "eternally feminine leading us upwards and on," wisdom is an inspiration on the path of realization. In the *Jerusalem Bible*, wisdom is the teacher providing knowledge of all the elements, aspects, and processes of the cosmos. Similarly, in the *Book of Proverbs*, wisdom exists even before the conception of light, and not even darkness can triumph over her. Among the ancient Greeks, Athena, the god-

48. Queen Dedes as Prajnaparamita. Java, 13th century.

dess of wisdom, presided over the moral and intellectual aspects of human life. From her were derived all the products of wisdom and understanding, all the arts and sciences, whether of peace or war. In the Buddhist tradition, *Prajnaparamita*, transcendent knowledge, is the Mother of all the Buddhas, she who gives birth to the Victorious Ones—those who penetrate the veils of ignorance and attain full enlightenment.

The wisdom that these mother-goddess figures personify can only be realized through personal and inner awakening. One could easily think, mistakenly, that the wisdom of the feminine is an external reality, something to be found outside, for it is difficult to recognize and accept that this powerful force of knowing is a part of our basic human heritage or nature. Looking for wisdom outside of oneself gives rise to the labyrinth of confusion and intelligence; one creates an external goal that can never be realized because one is looking for it in the wrong place. At the same time, making the journey through the labyrinthine path of developing intelligence is a worthwhile goal in itself. One may have the suspicion that one's labyrinth has no substantial reality at all except as a projection of the struggle of confusion and insight. Yet this maze—experienced as moments of doubt, clarity, and inspiration—is all that one has. Although working with the mundane forms of hope and fear, intelligence and confusion, cannot lead directly to wisdom, by traveling this labyrinth one can nevertheless discover the transition from outer to inner that does reveal true wisdom.

Being timeless, wisdom destroys the idea of itself as even an inner goal; being spontaneous, it happens nowhere else but in the continually occurring present. In journeying through the labyrinth it may finally occur to one that wisdom completely pervades the space in which one lives, and the intriguing possibility that one is already fully united with wisdom then presents itself. Though the potential of this realization provides profound inspiration, in one's daily life it is difficult to remember, much less actualize.

On the other hand, one may believe that the labyrinth is not of one's own making and that, therefore, one is not responsible for the obstacles life may present. One may conclude that there is an external agent or force that created the labyrinth and that can provide salvation from its tortuous route. Or, one may think that this confusing maze is simply in the given nature of things, a product of fate before which one is essentially alienated and helpless.

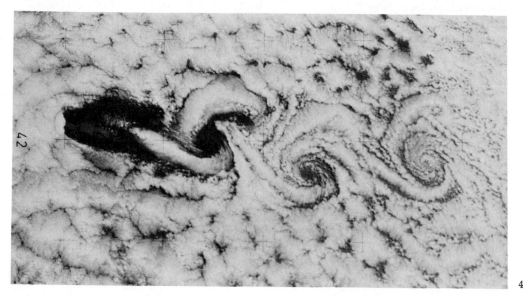

49.   Clouds off Baja.

Holding to these attitudes one remains as a child, nursed by self-centered beliefs about the world. An arbiter, translator, power, or god is sought, who can set things straight and to whom all problems can be referred. In expecting this sort of external intervention, one is like a child clutching at its mother's skirt, hoping that she will take care of things. As long as she either nurses or spanks, one need not fear; mother is tending to one's intimate needs and difficulties. This attraction for the warmth and safety of home and the fear of leaving it actually exaggerate the estrangement from the world. Why? For while one feels that one is grasping at the coattails of the world for protection, one has actually created a barrier that separates one from the reality of existence.

Another attitude one may have is the feeling of being deprived of ultimate security. This attitude, coupled with the nostalgia for the comfort of a womblike atmosphere, may give rise to the experience of helplessness in the midst of life, of suffering the bitter wound of separation. The sense of impotence can grow into a belief that one was born into a world one never made. Feeling utterly hopeless, one may declare that there is no exit or relief from the meaninglessness of the empty and dispassionate world. One's claustrophobia and despair could push one to realize the emptiness and intelligence of confusion. But, rather than relating with the potential spaciousness of emptiness, one is more likely to recoil in anger and self-pity.

Like a crying child looking over the precipice of bewilderment and intelligence, one sees nothing but an abyss of fear. Finding it difficult to let go of one's alienation, one makes a home in anger, weariness, cynicism, or despair. Paradoxically, although one experiences the reality of aloneness—having been ejected from the womb and its cozy childhood world—one still remains as an angry child, pouting and resenting its mother and struggling against the wrathful father figure.

The belief that one's confusion has been caused by an external agent or is the result of being born into a world dominated by an alien force reflects the potential for bewilderment evoked by the twists and turns of the labyrinth. As the play of solidity and emptiness, disappointment and hope, desire and satiation, life's dynamic maze is the playful expression of feminine and masculine. The feminine throws out her magical thread, weaving a seductive veil that challenges and inspires the heroic action of the masculine, who travels through the labyrinth in search of the wisdom of the feminine.

Although one may be seduced by the feminine or perhaps threatened by her elusive ways, one can learn from her play rather than remaining stuck in the labyrinth of her trickery and one's own confusion. The pursuit of feminine wisdom depends upon an appreciation of the playfulness of everyday situations, the whimsy of the unexpected, and the humor peeking through the contrast of moods and thoughts.

A particularly expressive personification of the feminine trickster is the *dakini*, whose Sanskrit name literally means "sky walker" or "sky being." In the Vajrayana Buddhist tradition she represents the direct experience of the fleeting and pulsing manifestations of the unborn feminine. The energy of

50. Caddoon pottery water bottle. Louisiana, 1300-1700 A.D.

51. Dakini. Nepal, 17th-18th century.

phenomenal experience that she embodies is no different than pure knowledge or primal intelligence. Often depicted as a simultaneously seductive and
terrifying female being, she mocks and destroys expectations while displaying
the possibility of open awareness. The dakini plays with the force and hunger
of passions, humors one's belief in self-importance, and delights in one's lack
of self-esteem. In so doing, she not only destroys confusion but points to or
indicates the path of developing insight. A particularly disruptive or disturb-
ing experience might challenge or destroy the solidity of one's beliefs or sense

55

of being. There is a gap or a moment in which there is a choice: either to continue to hold onto one's outlook or to view this seemingly chaotic experience as some kind of message or intelligence communicated by the environment. Although life situations are not always so dramatic or destructive, the possibility to transcend self-importance and to see clearly, as the play of the dakini, is always presenting itself. Whether or not one allows oneself to be tricked or seduced, the entire atmosphere of the situation is permeated with intelligence.

The hero, provoked to find intelligence and strength and to act upon it through the experience of openness and aloneness, embodies the qualities of the masculine. The hero is the son and lover treading the labyrinthine path of bewilderment and intelligence. Whether hero or heroine, the overall nature of the heroic quest is a function of our masculine aspect responding to and articulating its own nature as reflected in the spaciousness and wisdom of the feminine. Depending on whether one is a man or a woman, the nature of the quest may take on a different outer appearance. Yet the pattern of the heroic path is similar: pain, bewilderment, seeking, initiation, discipline, and finally, the attainment of knowledge.

What sustains this heroic movement and activity is not the idea of reaching a particular goal but the pervasive insight provided by one's repeated contact and communication with wisdom, which proclaims the sanctity of the present moment and the ordinary yet unconditioned majesty of reality. In coming to appreciate the clarity and power of immediate experience, the labyrinthine boundaries at last dissolve. The marriage of openness and clarity creates a spontaneous joy. One can then continue one's journey on the path; taking another step is no problem. For if one can see clearly, one finds that the world is already presenting the footprints to follow.

52. The labyrinthine face of Khumbaba, the monster encountered by the Sumerian hero, Gilgamesh, in the depths of the forest journey.

53. The pursuit of wisdom.

54. Sculpted Olmec head symbolizing the birth of awareness from the body of the earth mother.

CHAPTER FIVE
The Shape of History

HISTORY DISPLAYS THE SAME labyrinthine quality and struggle for the attainment of knowledge as the individual life journey. The nature and course of history can be read in the highlights of events, the development of structural motifs, and the variations of our use and understanding of basic symbols. The composite pattern of human actions, of constructive and destructive drives, and the numerous forms of human expression all articulate the environmental space of history, which, like the matrix of the feminine, is rich in its possibilities for inspiring and challenging us.

There is no precise point in time when history began. Out of the predawn hours of human development certain basic roles and attitudes emerged. The virgin environment was venerated in ritual and symbol and was recognized as a palpable living medium from which nourishment could be gathered and knowledge gleaned. With a mixture of profound reverence, awe, and fear, our ancestors learned to shape and articulate their world through the development of fire and the fashioning of delicate stone implements. At either end of the spectrum of primitive life lay the eternal mysteries of birth and death, both of which seemed intimately connected to the vast unknown. Life was viewed and experienced as a ceaseless round, going from the womb of birth to the womb of death, all contained within the maternal embrace of earth and endless space.

Earth burial and the later development of cave sanctuaries were forms of tribute to the mystery of the forces of the world. In the caves deep within the earth, the great dramas of birth, nourishment, hunting, and death were celebrated and ritually enacted. Intuitive awareness of rebirth and renewal could have been sparked whenever one emerged from the torchlit darkness of the cave to confront the actualities of life and the struggle for existence. In the world of our cave-dwelling ancestors, the demands of the physical environment and the continual and often difficult search for food transformed the receiving of nourishment into a central focus of magic and ritual. Sorcery and shamanism were born from the ritual reenactment of the life and death of the deer, the bison, the bear, or the jaguar. These rites offered the community a mystical participation in the greater round of life and death and were intended to ensure the continued provision of food.

55. Goddess in mouth of cave. Olmec.

THE FEMININE   The whole of nature was perceived as a fertile woman giving birth to all forms of life; her breasts were ripe with the sweetness of the world. One finds this personification of the all-embracing and accommodating power of the world in the goddesses drawn and sculpted by our early ancestors. Accompanying the growing belief in a Great Mother or a Great Goddess were subsidiary goddesses of bird, bear, fish, bee, frog, tree, and other nature cults. The growing psychological and social sophistication of the late Stone Age was reflected in increasingly intricate symbolic forms and artistic representations of the phenomenal world. Sanctuaries devoted to the worship of the Great Mother were created, venerating her power over birth and death and the ongoing processes of the universe.

56.

57.   Mistress of the animals. Greece, 700 B.C.

Slowly, the fertile and multitextured world space began to yield its secrets and knowledge. As primitive peoples began to explore the workings of nature, a rich and expanded world of symbolic forms developed out of their observations of such phenomena as the annual cycle of plants, the rising and setting of the sun, the appearance, disappearance, and reappearance of the moon, and the ebb and flow of the tides and the seasonal waters. In their depictions of their world, our ancestors used the symbols derived from these organic processes to describe an enriched and intense relationship with the primordial environment.

A great collective rite of passage occurred with the agricultural revolution, which began at different points in time and over a period of several millennia spread across a large part of the world. To tame the humble plant sprouting from earth's fertile womb required a total reorganization of human energy. The entire field of knowledge was expanded and transformed when human beings focused their attention on understanding the growth cycles of plants and on coordinating this with the patterns and movements of celestial bodies. Harnessing this knowledge produced a relatively stable source of food for

58.

60

59.

humankind. The development of agriculture was accompanied by the domestication of animals, the slow development of metallurgy, and the refinement of tools and weapons, which brought in their wake far-reaching changes in social and cultural life. The alterations in the orientation of human understanding introduced new and more precise articulations of space—whether in the patterns of fields and irrigation canals or in the spiritual enrichment and expansion of community life.

With the growth in social organization, a small number of villages developed into urban centers that were considered focal points of cosmic as well as human energy. Pyramids, and other structures recalling the sacred mountain of primal origins, and long ceremonial avenues flanked by geometrically precise temples were constructed in the early sites to accommodate sumptuous and elaborate rituals. These sacred structures throughout the world shared remarkable similarities in form. Along the banks of the Nile and the Euphrates, in the Indus river valley, among the alluvial plains of China, and in the semiarid highlands of Mexico, priests, priestesses, and astronomers coordinated the relationships between earth, heaven, and human beings and

60. Catal Hüyük shrine.

61

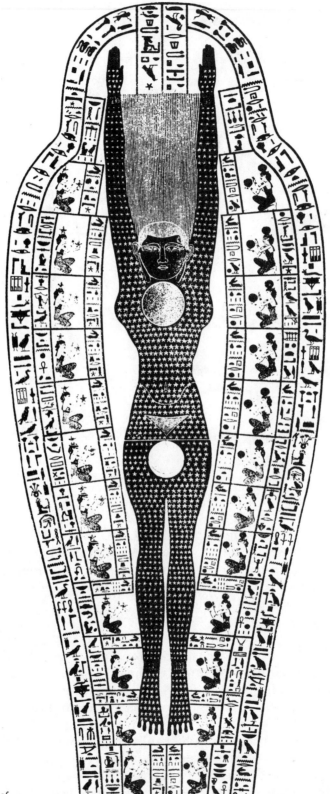

61.   Nut. Sarcophagus relief.

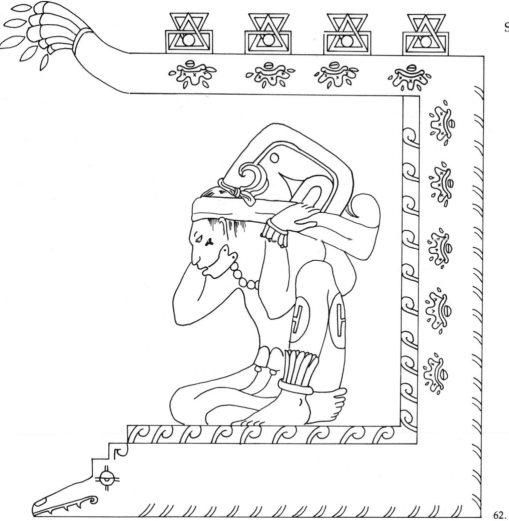

62. Mayan Time Bearer.

their destinies. In the early agricultural urban centers, complex calendars, precise astronomical calculations, and intricate symbolic languages were developed. Underlying the search for accurate conceptualizations and abstractions to describe natural laws and human experience were the primordial concerns that have always been presented by the bewildering contrast of empty space and its multitudinous forms: who are we, where did we come from, and where are we going? As society and thought developed more sophisticated patterns, the mysteries only seemed to deepen.

The sky with its heavenly bodies and their various movements became a richly layered metaphor for the space intimately connected with the mysteries of birth, growth, and death. Among the Egyptians, the all-encompassing celestial expanse was identified with the goddess Nut, whose star-emblazoned body embraced and nourished the earth and gave birth to the gods and goddesses. In ancient Mexico the symbolism for the rites of death and rebirth was provided by observations of the planet Venus' fragile oscillations through the vast nocturnal sky.

63

Like their Stone Age forebears, the citizens of the great agricultural civilizations continued the traditions of burial and expanded the attendant ceremonies to include the construction of monumental tombs. If anything, the fascination with the mystery of death only increased with the development of agriculture. The basic attitude echoed the original presentiment that death was an initiation into a complete knowledge of primordial space. From the earliest Stone Age well into historical times, the corpse frequently was placed in the foetal position, expressing the belief that death is a return to a ceaselessly receptive and generative mother. In burying their royal dead beneath pyramids—the symbol of the cosmic mountain—the Egyptians and Mayans continued the symbolism represented by early cave sanctuaries that had been thought of as the womb of the earth.

From time immemorial, the voyage of the dead, like life's journey, has been thought to be attended by tests and initiatory encounters. *The Tibetan Book of the Dead* is among the most sophisticated of the few surviving texts that describe the passage of the dead. It has been characterized in traditional commentaries as a "book of space" and describes the encounter with death as a fundamental experience of unborn feminine space. The possibility of attainment of ultimate knowledge in the after-death state is described as a merging or meeting of the "son mind"—the recently deceased—with the "mother mind"—primordial space and intelligence.

The highly developed rites and mysteries of the dead that were celebrated during the early period of the agricultural revolution cannot be construed as merely morbid or primitive sensibilities. The intuition that death leads to knowledge of the generative and renewing powers of universal space gave birth to highly sophisticated attempts to build structures that would reflect the majesty of the cosmos. The early builders desired to construct a living image of the timeless realm of the cosmic womb. Thus architecture, the mother of the arts, was born.

By giving shape and boundary to boundless space, architecture provides a basic arena for human creativity. It is the interplay of the feminine—providing ceaseless space and inspiring intelligence—and the masculine—responding with skillful and ingenious means. Through architecture, numerous human abilities are challenged, developed, and brought together. Knowledge of mathematics, geometry, physics, astronomy, and the laws of proportions are joined to the stonemason's skill in cutting and fitting; these are finished with the narrative and ornamental flourish provided by the woodworker, the painter, the glazer, the jeweler, and the metal worker, each representing one of the newly developed craft guilds. The coordination of human activity required for the construction of major architectural projects was mirrored in the proliferation of intricate pantheons of gods and goddesses inhabiting hierarchical realms of celestial and infernal space. The numerous deities not only reflected perceptions of the external world but also began to personify subtle nuances of emotional, spiritual, and intellectual life. Many of these deities are still remembered, enshrined in myths of death and resurrection and in stories

64

of their legendary journeys. From this period in the ancient Middle East, the Mediterranean, India, Asia, the Pacific, and the Americas come the familiar names of Astarte, Osiris, Dionysius, Brahma, Shiva, Amataresu, Maui, Quetzalcoatl, Coatlicue, and many others.

63. Egyptian bas-relief depicting the enactment of the mysteries of life and death.

THE FEMININE   Each deity had to be properly propitiated with particular acts and implements, typifying a tendency toward specialization and resulting in a new emphasis on the uniqueness of individual existence. Although the cult of the Great Goddess or Great Mother continued through the entire period of the agricultural revolution, it slowly diminished in importance or was absorbed into new cults. Deities like Isis, Diana of Ephesus, and Demeter personified a primary generative potency; the muses became the patronesses of the arts; goddesses such as Kali, the Greek fates, and the Mayan Ixchel presided over the energies of destruction. Growing from cults of the goddess and the mysteries of the dead, schools of metaphysical thought began to develop. Throughout the ancient world, philosophy was born, with its speculative investigations penetrating into the meaning of life, death, and the nature of mind.

I am everything that was, that is, that shall be . . .
Nor has any mortal ever been able to discover what lies under my veil.
                    Inscription on the base of a statue of Isis in the city of Saïs

Originally philosophy—literally meaning the love of wisdom—grew from a sense of bewilderment and questioning brought about by the elaborateness of the great cosmological pantheons and the increasing complexity of civilization. The intricate refinement of conception underlying the agricultural cosmologies inspired further philosophical attempts to synthesize and simplify the understanding of the ultimate nature of things. In these philosophical questionings, there was a concern for regaining and reintegrating into present-day life the primordial condition or experience that originally gave birth to the evolving structures of civilization.

Wherever philosophy developed, its goal was the attainment of wisdom, which was often identified with some quality or aspect of the feminine. The realization of wisdom was associated with regaining an appreciation of the original, nondual nature of reality, and this understanding was considered to be the basis for leading a fully awakened life. Among the Pythagoreans, wisdom was envisioned as an all-embracing feminine world soul. The Taoists in China emphasized the reestablishment of wisdom within oneself as a "clinging to the female."

The world had a beginning
And this beginning could be called the mother of the world.
When you have known the mother
Go on to know the child.
After you have known the child
Go back to holding fast to the mother,
And to the end of your days you will not meet with danger.
                    Lao Tzu

66

64. World deluge presided over by the Old Goddess, Ixchel. Mayan.

65.

Whether known as the *Hagia Sophia* of the Christians, *Anima Mundi*, the world soul of the alchemists, or *Prajnaparamita*, the transcendent knowledge of the Buddhists, the great legacy of the early philosophers is the understanding of the feminine nature of wisdom.

As the feminine became internalized as wisdom, its outer symbolic form was increasingly associated with the moon and earth. At the same time, coincident with the rise of patriarchy, male deities became increasingly associated with the sky and the heavenly realms, usurping the primordial domain of the feminine. The highest celestial regions, now often populated and nearly always governed by masculine deities, were understood as the source of wordly power and authority, thereby legitimizing the growing tendencies toward patriarchy and male supremacy.

As agricultural societies became more specialized, and patterns developed of rising and falling civilizations, highlighted by conditions of rebellion and war, there was a marked shift toward partriarchy. It is a highly debated issue whether or not patriarchy was preceded by a longstanding, universal, and generally peaceful matriarchy. Whatever the case, the development of patriarchy is one of the pivotal psychological revolutions in human history. Although patriarchy became dominant at the same time as the rise of agricultural societies, we cannot conclude that the two are necessarily or causally related. Many patriarchal groups, such as certain North American Indian and African tribes, are hunters or live in a marginal agricultural situation. Conversely, there are a few groups in a late hunting and early agricultural stage of development that still are generally matriarchal. Even where patriarchy is the rule, tribal values often emphasize the magical, mystical, and intuitive. The rituals relating community life to the environment are rooted in a perception of the universe as basically feminine: earth as the cosmic womb and space or sky as the unending begetter of the forms of life, both interwoven with goddesses presiding over the cycles of existence.

The distinguished and controversial German historian Oswald Spengler made the intriguing comment that men make history while women *are* history. Spengler's theory asserts that at some undetermined point in the transition from tribal life to urban existence, men felt left out of the biological rhythms and processes of womankind. To compensate for their isolation, men presumably began to aggressively assert and exclusively identify with the masculine element of their being. Spengler further assumed that women, identifying solely with the feminine element, felt that they contained everything, that they were already "it," and had no need to go out and prove themselves. What this theory points to is the problem of exclusive identification, of men with the masculine and women with the feminine principle. The problem of chauvinism and its consequent distortions in the panorama of modern history arise from such overidentification.

In the more developed agricultural civilizations, such as Imperial Rome and Han Dynasty China, the trend toward patriarchy led to the development of both bureaucracy and individualism. Societies were organized into different craft guilds, mercantile groups, political ruling classes, and armies. The increasing emphasis on the values of cleverness and self-assertiveness put the individual in a unique situation. Weaving one's way through intricate social patterns, one could rise to a position of worldly power and influence, or by the same token, one could experience more acutely the isolation of one's life.

Sensitive to both the potentiality and fragility of existence, the individual became ripe for the development of new spiritual traditions. In the great and colorful marketplaces and bazaars of the ancient world, amidst the mingling of merchants and soldiers, courtesans and princes, between the incantations of the old cults and the questionings of the philosophers, the new religions were born. Their emphasis was not so much on establishing another god or cult, as on illuminating the individual's relation to the unique space of his or her own destiny or to some ultimate god or creator.

66. Prehistoric Japanese figurine displaying the inherent rhythms of energy attributed to the feminine.

69

67. Shinto female deity.

Buddhism, Christianity, and Islam, responding specifically to these needs, developed into international religions, embracing and overcoming cultural differences. Judaism, Hinduism, and Taoism, growing from older tribal religions, in the course of time also spoke to the individual's quest for orientation and meaning in the face of the complexities of civilization and the bewildering immensity pointed to by the questions of birth and death.

At the core of all of these traditions is the philosophical concern with wisdom. There was a need for a reevaluation of the relationship between oneself and the world, searching for a deeper articulation and enrichment of inner life and the space of the mind. Beginning with Buddhism, and spreading to Christianity and Taosim, monasticism grew directly out of the emphasis on the value of introspectively exploring the psychological space of one's

70

inherent aloneness. As a new social element, the monastic orders were contemplative communities of men and women committed to understanding their own aloneness and developing compassion toward themselves, society, and the world as a whole. One of the unique features of traditional monasticism is the separation of the sexes. Although wishing to be away from the opposite sex is a legitimate exercise of one's freedom, the division of the monastic orders into monasteries and nunneries may have also reflected the chauvinism and dogmatism ingrained in patriarchal society.

Because the new religions also developed in response to the bewilderments of urban living, social breakdown, feudal warfare, and invasions, the concern for wisdom was often lost in the effort to provide a tangible alternative to the practical and material sense of claustrophobia and insecurity that many citizens of this age experienced. The hunger and desire for a more compassionate and eternal space was answered by promises of heaven, paradise, or everlasting life. Particularly in the literature of Christianity, Buddhism, and Islam, there are descriptions of paradises filled with every possibility of happiness, sensual enjoyment, and immortality, which awaited the faithful and would end their material and psychological suffering.

The growth of the universal religions added to an already expanding spatial sensibility. The devastations of war, whose motivation was often a distortion of religious zeal, did not deter the growth of commerce and in fact added to the contact among peoples and their ideas. Merchants and soldiers were accompanied and often preceded by traveling monks, nuns, and wandering scholars, who set up great networks of communication and learning. Architecture also came into renewed prominence with the rise of the political and economic power of the major religions.

Related to the pyramid of Egypt and the ziggurat of the ancient Middle East is the Buddhist stupa, a rounded earthwork derived from the tombs of ancient Indian kings. The stupa typifies the spatial sensibility characteristic of this age and became endowed with a very elaborate symbolism and set of cosmic associations. According to the specifications given by the Buddha, the stupa was always to be built at an important crossroad as a commemorative reminder of the teaching of enlightenment. The four gates leading to the stupa symbolize the four main events in the life of the Buddha: to the east his birth; to the south his enlightenment; to the west his teaching or turning of the wheel of the law; and to the north his Parinirvana or death. The ground plan of the entry gates forms the four bent arms of a swastika. By circumambulating the stupa, the Buddhist practitioner could reexperience the life of the Buddha and the stages of enlightenment. Similar to the older pyramids of Egypt, the stupa, like a giant breast, is also the image of the earth or cosmic womb, containing at its center a relic, often a bone of the Buddha or of some important monk or nun. The Pali name given to this form—*dagoba*—literally means the womb of space. As the chief architectural symbol of enlightenment, the stupa epitomizes the attainment of wisdom as the experience of unborn feminine space.

68. Dagoba. Anuradhapura, Ceylon. 1st century B.C.

71

69. Stupa. Tissamaharama, Ceylon.

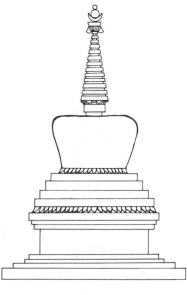

70. Chöten.

Through its long history the stupa has undergone a number of structural changes. In Southeast Asia and Java it was transformed into an elaborate pyramidal form; in China and Japan it developed into the elongated form of the pagoda; and in Tibet it became the vertical arrangement of geometrical forms known as the *chöten*. In all of its varied forms the stupa has remained a highly symbolic reference point articulating physical space and expressing the psychological condition of the awakened state of mind.

The Christian and Islamic architectural traditions have also developed monuments that articulate a similar approach to the landscape of terrestrial space. One of the unique contributions of these religions to architecture has been their elaborate construction of buildings that heighten awareness of interior space. The pyramid and stupa did contain an inner sanctum or tomb, but the Christian cathedral and Islamic mosque provide an expanded and public interior space, augmented by a wealth of symbolic meanings. The concept of a rounded interior architectural space certainly was not the exclusive property of Islamic and Christian societies. In fact, it may have originated with the cave meditation halls created by Buddhists and Jains in India and Central Asia. These cave temples may well have inspired the cave monasteries

72

71. The Hagia Sophia Mosque, Istanbul.

of the proto-Christian Essenes along the river Jordan. The full structural development of the cathedral and mosque interior space was made possible by the Roman invention of the true arch and the dome. However, it was the spiritual sensibilities of Islam and Christianity that informed the development of their architecture and infused it with an unmatched appreciation for the sacredness of interior space.

The early Christian domes and solidly arched naves created a large protective and inspired womb space, reflecting the totality of cosmic creation. As the cathedral developed during the flowering of Christianity in Europe, it took on the full dimensions of being both an interior vault of the universe and an external cosmic point of reference. Echoing the breast-shaped stupa or domed Byzantine cathedrals, the mosque also developed simultaneously as a harmonious projection upon the terrestial landscape and an all-accommodating and inspiring interior space.

In Islam and Christianity architectural developments also reflected the popular presentation of a heaven or paradise that could be attained after the present life. The mosques, with their dazzlingly intricate geometric arabesques, symbolizing the starry sky and the all-encompassing invisible space extending infinitely beyond, and the Gothic cathedrals, with their soaring naves flooded with supernal colors of stained glass, were revelations of the paradise that awaited the faithful.

Behind the spectacular appeal of these architectural accomplishments was a unique and highly inspired synthesis of worldly knowledge and spiritual aspiration. To the builders and initiates of the inner teachings of these two faiths, the flood of light pouring from on high through the windows or aper-

72. The Mihrimah Sultan Mosque Turkey.

tures of the structures had an immediately transcendental function: to lead the contemplative beholder to a direct perception of the ineffable source of all harmony and radiance.

> *When—out of my delight in the beauty of the house of God—the loveliness of the many-colored stones has called me away from external cares, and worthy meditation has induced me to reflect, transferring that which is material to that which is immaterial, on the diversity of the sacred virtues: then it seems to me that I see myself dwelling, as it were, in some strange region of the universe which neither exists entirely in the slime of the earth nor entirely in the purity of Heaven; and that, by the grace of God, I can be transported from this inferior to that higher world in an anagogical manner.*
>
> Abbot Suger of St.-Denis

73.   Amiens Cathedral, France.

THE SHAPE OF HISTORY

A visual essay depicting basic forms and shapes that have articulated the space of human experience.

From Cave to Sanctuary

1. Cave sanctuary. Les Combarelles, France, 25,000 B.C.

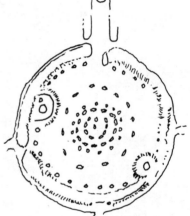

11. Corbelled Hillside tomb. New Grange, Ireland, second millennium B.C. Cross-section.

7. Great Mother temple. Gigantea, Malta, third millennium B.C. Ground plan.

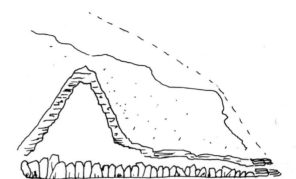

10. Observatory. Stonehenge, England, second millennium B.C. Ground plan.

2. Ceremonial earth chamber. Maes Howe, Orkney Isles, second millennium B.C. Cross-section and ground plan.

8. Kiva. Pueblo Bonito, North America, 12th-13th century. Ground plan.

9. Observatory. Stonehenge, England, second millennium B.C.

3. Eskimo igloo. North American Arctic. Cross-section.

4. Earth lodge. Pawnee, North American, 19th century. Cross-section.

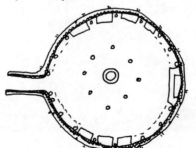

5. Earth lodge. Pawnee, North America, 19th century. Ground plan.

6. Passage grave. Kercade, Britanny second millennium B.C. Ground plan.

From Mountain to Temple

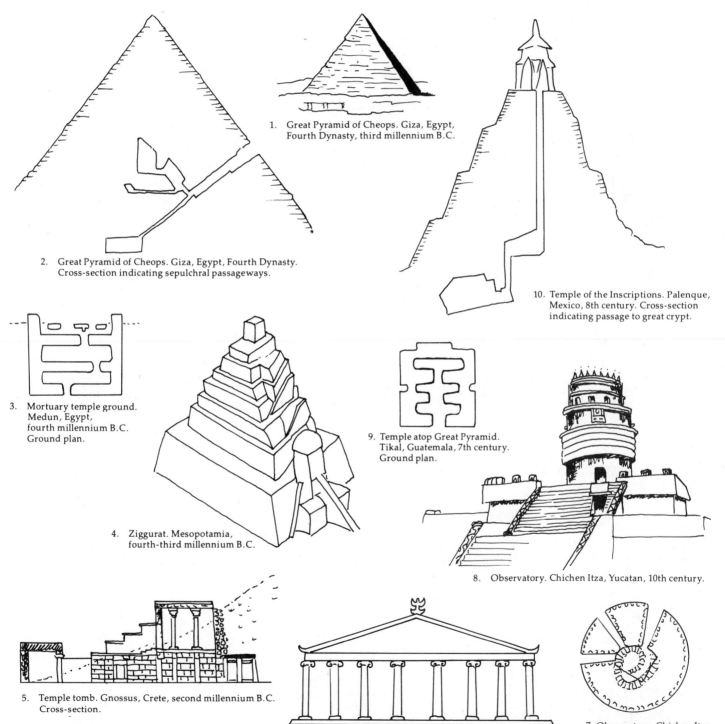

1. Great Pyramid of Cheops. Giza, Egypt, Fourth Dynasty, third millennium B.C.

2. Great Pyramid of Cheops. Giza, Egypt, Fourth Dynasty. Cross-section indicating sepulchral passageways.

10. Temple of the Inscriptions. Palenque, Mexico, 8th century. Cross-section indicating passage to great crypt.

3. Mortuary temple ground. Medun, Egypt, fourth millennium B.C. Ground plan.

4. Ziggurat. Mesopotamia, fourth-third millennium B.C.

9. Temple atop Great Pyramid. Tikal, Guatemala, 7th century. Ground plan.

8. Observatory. Chichen Itza, Yucatan, 10th century.

5. Temple tomb. Gnossus, Crete, second millennium B.C. Cross-section.

6. Temple of Artemis. Ephesus, Greece, 6th century B.C.

7. Observatory. Chichen Itza, Yucatan, 10th century. Cross-section.

From Womb to Dome

1. Daigo-ji pagoda. Kyoto, Japan, 10th century.

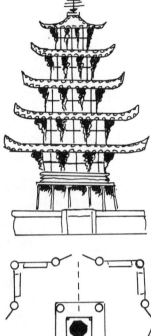

8. Néak Péan or lotus mountain tower growing from lake. Angkor Thom, Cambodia, 13th century.

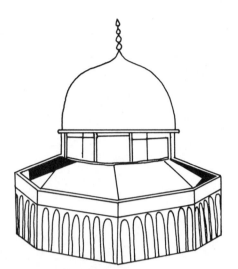

9. Dome of the Rock, so-called "Mosque of Umar." Jerusalem, Israel, 7th century.

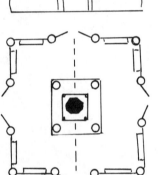

2. Daigo-ji pagoda. Kyoto, Japan, 10th century. Ground plan indicating mandala of two worlds: left, womb world; right, diamond world.

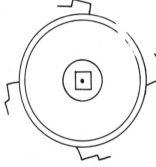

7. Great stupa. Sanchi, India, 2nd century B.C. Ground plan.

10. Jai Singh observatory. Delhi, India, 17th century.

3. Buddhist rock-cut cave temple and adjoining monastery. Bhaja, India, 2nd century B.C. Ground plan.

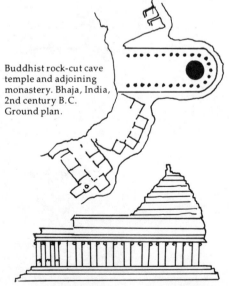

6. Great stupa. Sanchi, India, 2nd century B.C.

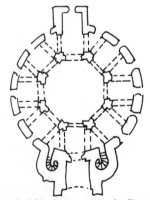

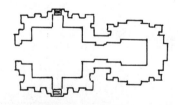

4. Dura temple. Aihole, India, 6th century.

5. Parasurameshavara temple. Bhuveneshvar, India, 8th century. Ground plan.

11. Chapel of Charlemagne. Aix-la-Chapelle, France, 8th century. Ground plan.

Opening to Unborn Space

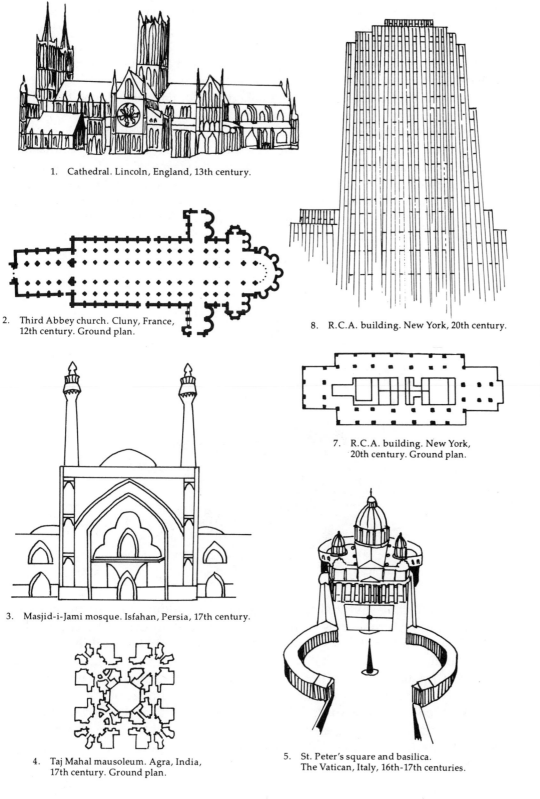

1. Cathedral. Lincoln, England, 13th century.

2. Third Abbey church. Cluny, France, 12th century. Ground plan.

3. Masjid-i-Jami mosque. Isfahan, Persia, 17th century.

4. Taj Mahal mausoleum. Agra, India, 17th century. Ground plan.

8. R.C.A. building. New York, 20th century.

7. R.C.A. building. New York, 20th century. Ground plan.

5. St. Peter's square and basilica. The Vatican, Italy, 16th-17th centuries.

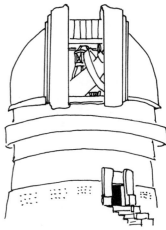

9. Orbiting space station with radio antennae and solar panels.

6. Observatory. Mount Palomar, California, 20th century.

During the great expansion of building, commercial enterprise, and military conquest that followed in the wake of the establishment of the world religions, wisdom slowly became the province of increasingly esoteric, mystical, or heretical schools of thought. Within the dynamic but conservatively patriarchal Islamic realm, the Sufis continued and elaborated upon the wisdom teachings and wordly knowledge of the ancient Mediterranean and Middle East. Cultivating a variety of ecstatic techniques, music, poetry, and art, the most inspired Sufi mystics often evoked wisdom as the beloved feminine with whom one must become indissolubly wed.

Early in the formation of the Christian Church, a highly centralized patriarchal orthodoxy was formed that excluded a number of schools emphasizing the Gnostic approach and the veneration of *Hagia Sophia,* Holy Wisdom. After the reintroduction of the knowledge of the ancient Mediterranean through prolonged contact with Islam, the Gnostic tradition in Christian Europe, though still maintained in some of the contemplative communities, developed largely in the hands of alchemists and related esoteric groups.

74.

Having officially divested itself of feminine wisdom, the Church needed the consoling maternal arms of the mother more than ever. The cult of the Virgin Mary, Mother of Christ, was developed, inspiring the Gothic tradition, the highpoint of Christian civilization. Embracing the infant Jesus, the Virgin provided Christians with an image of a great protective mother to whom they could pray and in whom they could seek refuge. The image of the Virgin was also identified directly with the "Mother" Church, which referred to itself in feminine terms. Projecting an outwardly maternal identity, the Church was able to maintain and perpetuate a patriarchal supremacy.

Instead of viewing the feminine as a Great Mother on whose lap one could remain, the alchemists' perception of the feminine was of an enticing wisdom whom one had to pursue and embrace, finally realizing her to be a part of one's essentially androgynous condition.

> *He who would enter the Kingdom of God must first enter with his body into his mother and there die.*
>
> Paracelsus

In Europe and the Middle East, Judaism, combining its own inspiration with influences of Islamic and Christian alchemy, developed the esoteric teachings of the Kabbalah. Symbolizing the tree of life and knowledge, the Kabbalah is an intricate system of thought that recognizes and works with the feminine and masculine principles as keys to the attainment of wisdom. The Hindu tantras also emphasize the interplay of the feminine *shakti* and the masculine *shiva* as a reflection of a nondual *(advaita)* point of view. Shakti is an active, creative energy and shiva a passive, spiritual energy. In the Taoist system, on the other hand, the feminine *yin* is characterized, above all, by a quality of receptivity and the masculine *yang* by an active, originating quality.

Buddhism, like the other major religions of the modern world, has developed along patriarchal lines that have tended to perpetuate its own militancy and restrictive dogmas. Not concerning itself with a primal creator or judge, however, the emphasis in all its major schools has been on the awakening of wisdom and the development of compassion in the individual. Particularly in the traditions of the Mahayana of China and Japan and the Vajrayana of Tibet, the space of the mind is explored through the basic practice of meditation, complemented by an emphasis on the study and practice of the wisdom teachings, epitomized in the *Prajnaparamita*. In the Buddhist conception, wisdom or transcendent knowledge, whose attainment is the crowning perfection of the path of enlightenment, is evoked by a number of feminine images: unborn space, the full moon, and the mother of intelligence.

Within the global development of present-day world civilization, fractured into ideologies and nationalities, each demanding its particular allegiance, the pursuit of wisdom has become like a persistent whisper. With the birth of modern science and the rise of industrialism, and its attendant material preoccupation, the individual has become caught up in a fast-moving yet confining space, often feeling an acute alienation from his or her own environment and the greater universe. In the words of William Blake, the individual loses his or her connection with the "starry dynamo of night."

In the industrialized world, space has been transformed by the development of mechanized transportation and electronic communications. While the landscape has been highly modified by freeways and sprawling urban growth, psychological space has been intensified and imploded by mass media such as television, radio, radar, and telephone. A distinctive architectural development of the present era is the skyscraper, which has its roots in the development of the tower. Originally conceived as a watchpost, taking the place of a mountain or a tree, the tower achieved great prominence in the fortresses and castles of feudal times. Piercing the sky, the spires and bell towers of Christian cathedrals and the minarets of Islamic mosques acquired the symbolic function of providing a celestial bastion to watch over the earth and call the faithful to prayer. Though differing greatly in purpose and possessing an unprecedented massiveness and height, the towerlike skyscrapers of the modern urban center nevertheless symbolize aspiring patriarchal authority that derives its power from its celestial proximity.

Due in part to the tremendous claustrophobia induced by the complexities of the contemporary world, we have launched into the exploration of outer space. This technological triumph has supported and complemented a reawakening of the revelatory instinct. The awe and wonder of the mysterious reaches of physical space inevitably lead back to questions concerning the nature of mind. The movement of history from the dark womb of the cave to the vast blackness of outer space reflects a labyrinthine journey from inner to outer and back again that is common to all of us.

The general lack of understanding, the suspicion and even hostility that surround the feminine in contemporary society attest to its inherent subtlety and trickiness. The current interest in and confusion about the meaning and implications of the feminine principle are also accompanied by renewed questioning of the nature of our being and our destiny on this planet. Undoubtedly similar feelings of confusion and mistrust were experienced at the dawn of agriculture, the birth of philosophy, the development of the great religions, and the genesis of modern science. The whole of our history developed from the intertwining of awareness and space. As awareness of our being in relation to the vast spaciousness of the world deepens and grows, there is a profound inspiration to refashion or shape this space. This is part of a self-generating process, engendering unforeseen or surprising consequences, which in turn inspire a further alertness and a deeper probing of the mysteries of life. Every major articulation of our intelligence gives birth to new structural patterns and forms that must encompass the cumulative effect of all of our previous actions.

Current interest in the feminine now seems to point to a new cycle of experience, bringing a more acute awareness of the mysteries and the splendors that are continually with us. The primordial power and insight of the feminine have been nourished by and feed, in return, the keepers of the portals of her domain. At moments barely flickering and at others bursting into flame, the inexhaustible space of the feminine continually ignites the generative spark of intelligence and imagination.

75.

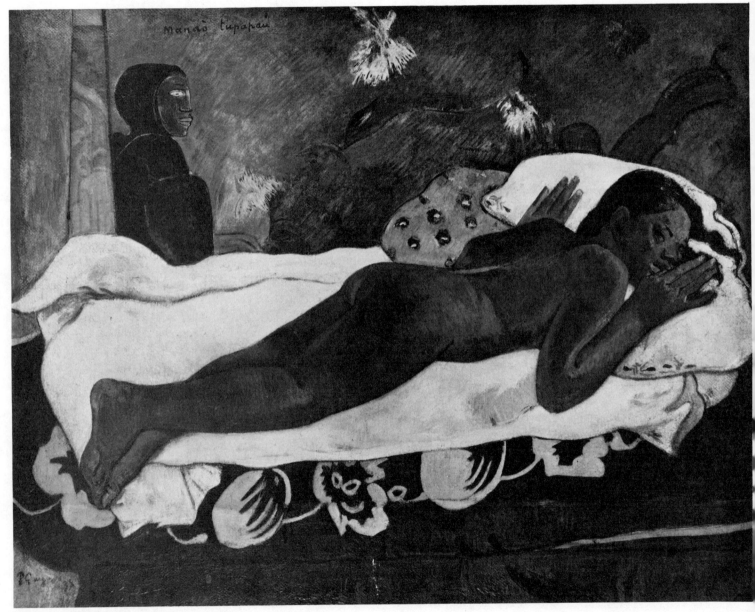

76. *Spirit of the Dead Watching*. Paul Gauguin.

CHAPTER SIX

Impermanence and the Middle Way

*Kaśyapa, the fact that the whole of reality is like celestial space
without any differentiating attributes, radiant and pure from its
very beginning, is the formation of an attitude directed toward
enlightenment.*

Buddha

THE INTUITION that the world of unceasing impermanence has a feminine
quality is universal. A popular image of the passing show of the world is that
of a voluptuous and seductive young woman. She may be gazing into a mirror
or staring at you with a beguiling gaze that reflects both innocence and lust.
With an inviting gesture she leads you on a dance that leaves you inebriated
and dazed, thirsting after a further taste of passion. Feeling the incomplete-
ness of the initial encounter, you continue the pursuit. After a number of mad
escapades, you catch up with your seductive hostess and finally have her all
to yourself. Now, the great moment. As you approach, she slowly disrobes,
and you begin to see—the flesh falling off her bones. Your young temptress
turns grey and shrivels up into an old hag. The stench of decomposition
chokes your throat so that you gasp for air. Reeling with terror, disgust, and
bewilderment, you tremble and rub your eyes, wondering if this is a dream
and, if it is, when it will end or how you can wake up.

The image of the decay of feminine beauty and youth expresses the powerful but frightening relationship of our passions or desires to impermanence.
The quickness of our passions and the spontaneity with which they arise all
too readily unmask us and remind us of our essentially impermanent nature.
Passion and our fear of passion, particularly our apprehensions about sexuality, reveal an extremely raw quality to life. If one succumbs to passion, one
fears that everything will be exposed, leaving one naked without pretense or
make-up. With no shelter, one is confronted with a nakedness that goes
beyond the sexuality of the situation itself. When passion uncovers the impermanence of our world, it is like seeing oneself without a face or name.
Existentially stark, one's encounters with desire can disclose the ruthless
breath of impermanence and emptiness, which one's individual mannerisms
and acquired cultural make-up attempt to conceal.

THE FEMININE

The sayings of the Preacher, *Ecclesiastes*, provide a popular heritage or folkwisdom on the theme of impermanence. To know that "to everything there is a season" becomes a balm for the perils and pitfalls of romantic love. Provocative insight into the shift and flux of things was also developed by the sixth-century philosophers of Ionian Greece, the most notable of whom was Heraclitus.

This universe, which is the same for all has not been made by any god or man, but it always has been, is, and will be—an ever-living fire, kindling itself by regular measures and going out by regular measures.

Heraclitus, *Fragments,* verse 29

The thinking of philosophers like Heraclitus, Pythagoras, and Anaximander on the fluid and continually transforming nature of things led to an introspective consideration of the nature of wisdom. In China a similar school of thought crystallized in the *I Ching*, whose binary symbols (—— and — —) point to the endless patterns of change in one's own psychological situation. The interaction of opposite energies or cosmic forces recognized by the Greek philosophers was developed by the Chinese into the principles of *yin*, feminine, and *yang*, masculine, and provided the basis in Chinese philosophy for a uniquely mathematical philosophy of impermanence. Like the Ionian Greeks, the Chinese, especially under the influence of Lao Tzu and Chuang Tzu, were inevitably led to a search for the wisdom within. In a famous text, Chuang Tzu described a dream in which he saw himself as a butterfly. When he awakened he asked himself whether at that moment he might not be a butterfly dreaming that he was a man. This questioning led him to consider the perplexities of the world of ceaseless change. Inspired by such bewilderment, the Taoists cultivated an inner stillness, the Tao, identified as the way underlying all change and transformation.

Investigating the nature of impermanence, the Vedic thought of early India, summarized in the *Upanishads*, arrived at an equally profound level of introspection. The world of impermanent appearances was described as *maya* and envisioned as a beguiling feminine creature in whose presence one should be extremely cautious. An ascetic ideal of life developed. Its goal was to attain union through the practice of austerities and sacrifices with the supreme cosmic force, the womb of all worlds, Brahman. Emphasis was placed on purification of the senses, sexual abstinence, withdrawal from life activity, and the cultivation of utter tranquility, whose resting point was the belief in a permanent soul, *atman*.

"Eat, drink, and be merry, for tomorrow we die!" The epicurean approach to the question of impermanence is a libidinous contrast to the ascetic ideal epitomized by the tradition of the *Upanishads*. The early Indian tradition and the epicurean approach seem to represent diametrically opposed responses to the questions posed by one's changing presence in the world: either one abandons the world or abandons oneself completely to the world.

77.

As a panorama of shifting scenes and events, now gaudy and ribald, now filling one's mouth with the taste of ashes, the world comes and goes, approaches and retreats, like a magical and fickle lover, whose enticements continually lead one to the brink of both glory and despair. One may rape or charm the world, love it or leave it, for who knows what the next day will bring? In viewing the world as an unpredictable lover who must be either abandoned or seduced, the ascetic and epicurean actually begin from a similar vision of change, although their responses to the question of impermanence lead in opposite directions. The epicurean denies anything beyond immediate sensory experience; the ascetic works at developing a complete indifference to sensory experience. Despite differences in their forms of expression, the epicurean and ascetic both emphasize an attitude of denial, either of the body or of any transcendent meaning, and therefore both could be described as nihilistic.

78.

80. *Dancing Skeleton*. José Posada.

Complementing the nihilistic approach to impermanence is the philosophy of eternalism. From this point of view, the question of impermanence is resolved by postulating an unchanging truth or reality, a reference point on which we can rely. This truth might be symbolized by belief in an unvarying god or in the absolute reality of some primal cause or ultimate end. An example is the analogy of Plato's cave, where the flickering, evanescent shadows of the everyday world are considered to be the play of an immortal and transcendent light whose source is beyond the cave, an eternal god or truth that lights up and gives meaning to the world of appearances. Though the eternalist may be enticed by the world, he or she may still be saved by placing faith in an immanent but eternal and transcendent god or absolute truth. The eternalist approach has often supported dogmatisms whose unyielding authority has given rise to static beliefs and social systems.

Eternalism and nihilism are two contrasting ways of seeing and dealing with the world of impermanence. Between these two attitudes there is a third traditional approach, a middle way that does not fixate on either asserting something above and beyond or rejecting altogether the reality of impermanence. The middle way as the classic mystical approach does not provide ultimate answers to the mysteries of change but rather represents a pragmatic approach to participating completely in the world while yet appreciating the sacredness of experience.

79. *Madonna*. Edvard Munch.

89

Creatures are subject to changing "states" but the gnostic has no "state" because his vestiges are effaced and his essence annihilated by the essence of another, and his traces are lost in another's traces.

Bāyazīd of Bistām, Persian Sufi

32. There is no cessation by means of itself; nor cessation by something other than itself; Just as there is no origination of origination by itself nor by another.

33. Because the existence of production, duration, and cessation is not proved, there is no composite product;
And if a composite product is not proved, how can a non-composite product be proved?

34. As a magic trick, a dream, or a fairy castle. Just so should we consider origination, duration, and cessation.

Nagarjuna, *Fundamentals of the Middle Way*

Beginning with a materialist and highly discriminating point of view that never totally lost sight of the reality of impermanence, modern physical science has also arrived at a point somewhere between the eternalist and nihilist positions. The once solid atomistic theory has been steadily eroded. Today the physicist is discovering a universe that is basically space in or upon which particles are created and decay, appearing and vanishing in rapid succession. The vacuous, featureless face of unborn space continues to present her vexing riddles to the laboratory scientist. This trickiness of the feminine was eloquently expressed in the words of physicist J. Robert Oppenheimer:

If we ask, for instance, whether the position of the electron remains the same, we must say "no"; if we ask whether the electron's position changes with time, we must say "no"; if we ask whether the electron is at rest, we must say "no"; if we ask whether it is in motion, we must say "no."

Science and the Common Understanding

The present-day image of the universe is that of a void-field of continually changing unfixable relationships, whether of particles or galaxies. According to one contemporary point of view, the Steady State Theory, matter is continually produced from nothing more than empty space. In fact, the very essence of the basic ingredient of the physical universe, the atom, is considered to be pure space that is dynamic and changing from moment to moment. The familiar theme of form and emptiness reasserts itself. The modern physical analysis of impermanence is largely theoretical: it is intellectually true but not necessarily experientially valid. How do we actually experience and come to understand the play of emptiness and form? How do we develop a living relationship with the impermanence and vastness of space?

The travels and feats of the hero and the mystic, described in traditional stories, myths, and folklore point to the journey one must make in order to accept impermanence and actualize unborn space. The theme of this journey is the interplay of the descent into and the emergence from the labyrinth of bewilderment and intelligence.

81. Microphotograph of a blood cell.

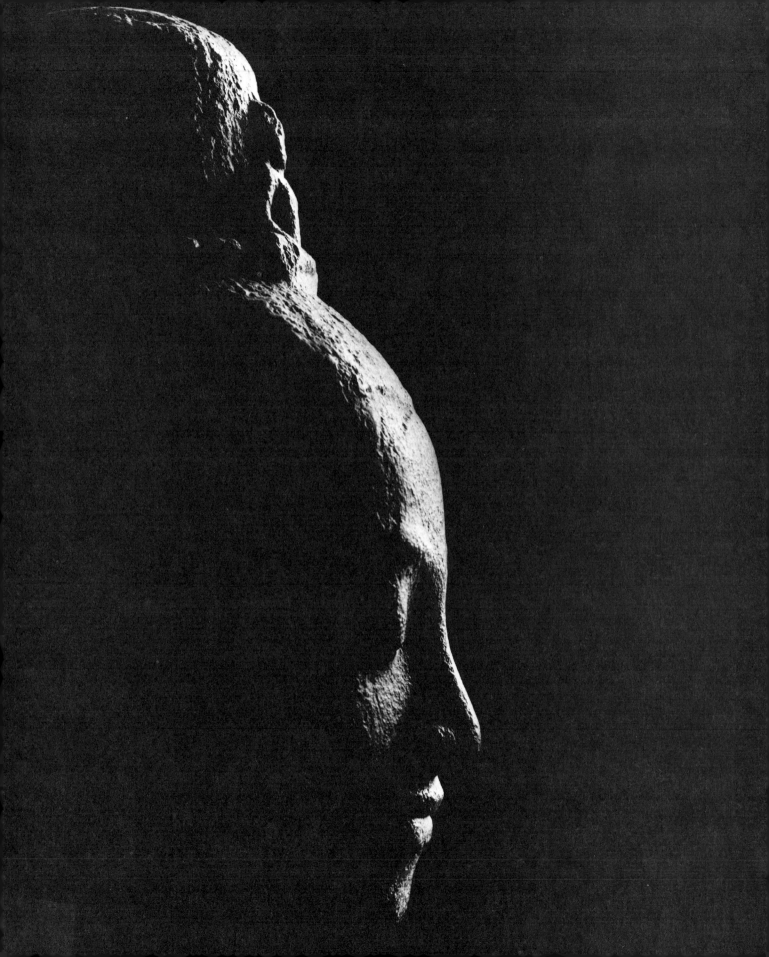

CHAPTER SEVEN
Unceasing Emergence

Thus the dead were addressed when they died ...
Awaken, already the sky is tinged with red,
Already the dawn has come,
Already the flame colored pheasants are singing,
The fire-colored swallows,
Already butterflies are on the wing ...

Song from Teotihuacan, Mexico

THE IMAGE OF DAYBREAK provides a powerful metaphor of the possibility of individual renewal and clarity of vision. The emergence from the darkness of one's own labyrinth is a transformative passage. As in birth, when one passes from an embryonic water-world to existence as an air-breathing child, so emergence is a sudden entry into a fresh, new world that needs to be communicated with and explored. Maternal comfort and the secure embrace of situations must eventually come to an end, and one is then ejected into a vast yet strangely familiar space.

The most powerful and obvious instances of emergence occur in dying and in birth. The recognition of emergence in everyday life, however, depends upon an appreciation of transitions and passages, the inevitable ruptures or fulfillments in situations and relationships that punctuate the flow of experience. In the world of desires, feelings, and expectations, we are continually experiencing death and birth, the two reference points of any initiation.

In the whole process of emergence, the initiation begins with a symbolic death, a giving up or submission that is also a symbolic return to the womb. The very acknowledgment of the labyrinthine quality of life plunges one into a womb of chaos. Chaos, like confusion, is a condition that can, by its very nature, cause one to be more alert and on one's toes as one experiences the shiftiness and turbulence of the energy of things. Whenever awareness is awakened by a sharp thrust of pain, or doubts and confusion are punctured by some unexpected jolt, a moment of clarity can occur, allowing one to glimpse the real nature of things.

Returned to an embryonic condition, enveloped in unborn space, naked of preconceptions or memories, one sees and experiences things as they are. Every event and thing expresses its inherent wholesomeness, which is nothing that is externally bestowed. Whatever is, is its own statement, what Meister Eckhardt described as "the isness of things." Realizing the inherent sacredness of things one is again ejected, reborn; one actually emerges into the only space there is.

Unconditioned space, without beginning or end, is inseparable from the experience of clarity that occurs in the midst of confusion. Clarity is a function equally of space and mind. Like a vast and bottomless arena of possibilities, mind is actually no different than the space that accommodates the cosmic dimensions of the universe. The perception may occur that the changing features of phenomena and situations are a reflection of the shiftiness of one's own mind. In these kinds of musings a spark occurs illuminating the link between one's intelligence and the nature of things. Because one has repeatedly experienced these momentary discoveries of the unconditioned womb of mind and space, one also knows, on one level, that it is continually there. Yet each time it feels fresh and new. If one surveys the panorama of individual life as well as of history, one begins to see the play of continual emergence.

The Pueblo Indian cosmography* of four successive underworlds illustrates the perception of unceasing emergence. Each world is contained within the Goddess Mother of creation from whom one is continually being reborn; whatever happens in life or death takes place within her womb of mind and space. Emerging from an underworld, it seems that one has entered into something different and unique, only to discover that one is yet in another underworld, never having left the womb of the Goddess Mother.

The whole atmosphere of life can be described as an underworld due to the inevitability of forgetfulness. We are continually forgetting who we are or why we are on this earth. When one emerges from forgetfulness, there is a quality of ascent. As if following a circular motion, the ascent leads to a regaining of the primordial understanding of one's origin and the possibility of entering into yet another underworld.

The four successive underworlds describe a life process leading to ever greater knowledge and wisdom, which is completely enveloped and supported by feminine space. In the Pueblo Indian myths echoing the origins of history, the beginning is a cave in the middle of which is the "Mountain of Generation." The imagery expresses the inseparability of feminine and masculine applied to one's personal life and to the cosmos. According to everyday assumptions, a cave is contained within a mountain, yet the Mountain of Generation is contained within a cave. The generative capacity of the masculine mountain comes from its own feminine quality—the cave that contains it.

The second world of emergence is described as "dark as is the night of a stormy season." Being located near the navel of the Earth Mother, it is called the "Umbilical-Womb of Place of Gestation." Here things literally take shape and begin to grow, and the awareness of extreme darkness creates the possibility of light. The third world, "like a valley in starlight," is called the "Vaginal-Womb or Place of Sex Generation." Here there is greater light and

*See Frank Waters's *Masked Gods.*

94

83. *The Ballantine*. 1948-1960. Franz Kline.

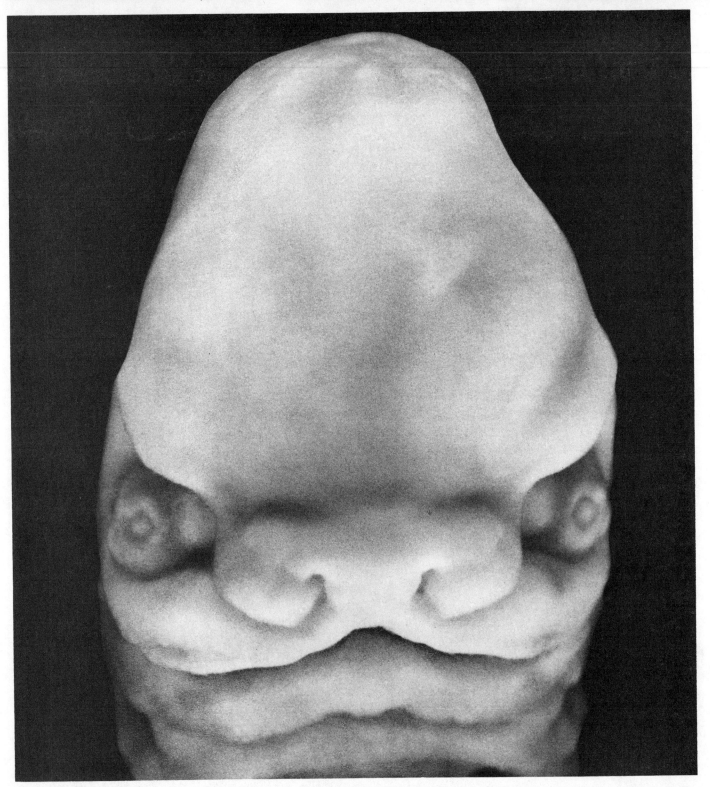

84. Face of 40-day human embryo.

thus greater discrimination. Described as the "Womb of Parturition," the fourth world is "light like the dawning." Reflecting the quality of enlightenment or emergence that is associated with rebirth, this realm is also called the "World of Disseminated Light and Knowledge or Seeing."

96

A tunnel or path runs through the center of the successive worlds. This the Hopi call *sipapu*. Like the life thread, the course of the breath, sipapu is an ongoing path inseparable from the unconditioned womb space of the feminine. Whatever we may call it—life's journey or destiny—there is some kind of path that each person pursues. The rhythmic flow of the path is itself reflected in the effort to find it or even remain on it, once one has found it. The pattern of lost and found, light and dark, asleep and awake, living and dying, is the expression of the unceasingness of the feminine and of our unceasing pursuit of its wisdom.

Embraced in darkness and radiating in rhythmic sequence its cool light, the moon sheds its fullness as a snake sloughs its skin. Displaying the unrelenting cycles and patterns of creation and destruction, waxing and waning, the moon has throughout history provided a symbol for the ever-renewing ceaselessness of the feminine. Far before the development of agriculture, the periodicity of the moon had been observed and venerated and was being translated into symbolic figures and notational systems, confirming the experience of time and the inevitability of impermanence. Correlations between the lunar cycle and menstruation inspired and enriched thought and rituals related to birth, death, and human destiny, mathematical conceptions, and the development of the arts.

The ancient Greeks perceived a dynamic potency in the moon when they envisioned the fates, the Moirae, as three women—a virgin, a matron, and an old hag—measuring our lives with their endless spinning and weaving. Among the Balinese the moon is depicted as a young woman energetically working at her spinning wheel within the mouth of a gigantic monster. Embracing and mocking human action, the devouring jaws of impermanence provide the cavernous home of the moon.

A common early myth about the moon focuses both on the impermanence of life and the theme of unceasing reemergence. The story begins as moon man, embodied as the waxing crescent moon, appears in the sky. He fights the spirit of darkness who had eaten his father during the previous lunar cycle. At the lunar zenith, moon man overpowers the monster and reigns over the earth in full glory, establishing order, agriculture, and social justice. However, his reign is brief; no sooner does he reach the peak of his power, then the monster begins to pursue him once again, gradually gnawing at him and reducing him to nothing. Moon man's death is the lunar dark period when he dwells in the underworld belly of the monster, while the earth undergoes a period of crisis and chaos. But moon man's fate is continual rebirth. As the dark phase subsides, his son once again emerges to resume the struggle.

Although taking on many different forms, evoking a myriad of mythic and psychological responses, the world of impermanence is inseparable from the womb of the mind or unborn space. The contrast between the world of change and the unconditioned, originless space of the mind is but the play of the relative and the absolute nature of reality. The wheel used for spinning is a symbol of impermanence and is also a symbol of completeness and cosmic totality.

THE FEMININE   The popular notion of the wheel of fortune, depicting the rising and falling of one's fate, is epitomized in Buddhist descriptions of *samsara,* the endless round of birth and death. The *Bhavachakra,* the Wheel of Endless Becoming, or Wheel of Life, is an iconographic summation of the Buddha's teaching of change. The wheel is held by the lord of death who rules over the world of change and decay. The hub of the wheel is turned by three animals—a rooster, a pig, and a snake—ceaselessly chasing each other. They represent, as they feed and prey upon each other, the emotions of passion, ignorance, and hatred. On the spokes of the wheel are drawings that represent different psychological conditions of suffering and bliss through which human consciousness is continuously passing. On the rim of the wheel are illustrations of the twelvefold law of interdependent origination, or cause and effect, which describes how our actions maintain and perpetuate the world of our expectations and preconceptions.

85. Wheel of Life
    (Bhavachakra), Tibet.

The paintings and relief carvings of the Wheel of Life are the earliest known visual teaching devices in the Buddhist tradition. They were used not only to point to the fundamental predicament or maze of confusion of human life, but also to attune the human mind to the unborn space or emptiness on which the wheel of change rests. Great spiritual traditions throughout history have developed similar teachings to point to the invisible ground of being that supports the world of becoming, the world of birth, death, and suffering.

Sufi, Kabbalistic, and Christian mystics speak of the poverty of God, of the nothing that is higher than God, or of God being the silence within us. Not limited by any name or attribute, God is the unconditioned experience through which one can know the supreme nature of things, even that which is beyond God. A certain Sufi fable relates the story of a king, who one day entered his royal court and observed one person who, among all those present, was not bowing down before him. Unnerved by the impudent act of this stranger in the back of the royal hall, the king cried out: "How dare you not bow down to me! Even my highest subjects bow down before me. Only God does not bow down before me, and there is nothing higher than God. Who then are you?" The tattered stranger answered with a smile, "I am that nothing."

The cultivation of the emptiness, silence, or nothingness that underlies and permeates all experience is no different than the development of wisdom. Being of the nature of space, wisdom and mind are of the same essence. To know and accept fundamental emptiness is to accept and come to know the nature of mind. A famous scholar once paid a visit to a Zen master, hoping to learn from him. After hearing the scholar's questions, the Zen master offered him tea. The visitor watched while the tea was being poured into the cup, overflowing it and finally splashing onto the table. The scholar, growing ever more aghast, cried out, "Stop! What are you doing! I thought you were enlightened, and you cannot even pour a cup of tea!" The Zen master stopped and replied, "This overflowing tea cup is like your mind when you came to visit me. Until you empty it, you will never learn anything."

Whatever forms or activities are involved in the process of emergence, the essential arena of activity is the mind. The emergence from confusion to clarity is a passage that requires the emptying of the mind. The process of emptying involves the development of an open attitude of working with the fundamental wholesomeness of things. The confused products of mind need not be feared when one realizes that in their innate nature they possess the emptiness and the wisdom of unborn space. Not afraid of losing something or being drained, the emergence from confusion to clarity is the disciplined actualization of emptiness.

The reality of emptiness does not mean that there is nothing in the world. However, whatever is there—whether a full moon, a bird flying in the sky, a memory or dream, or a well-stuffed armchair—is just a thing, a form that has no particular or fixed value. It is our aesthetic and utilitarian needs as well as our conceptions and behavior that define experience and lend uniqueness and

86. *Magnolia Blossom,* 1925. Imogen Cunningham.

value to our world. The meaning of emptiness, then, is not that the world is nonexistent or void, but that it is fundamentally open, that it can be interpreted, seen, or related to in many different ways.

If the world is empty of intrinsic meaning, impermanent and unceasingly in flux, then the forms that present themselves are also expressions of emptiness.

> *Form is emptiness, emptiness itself is form, emptiness is no other than form, form is no other than emptiness; in the same way feeling, perception, concept, and consciousness are emptiness.*

> Prajnaparamita, *The Sutra on the Essence of Transcendent Knowledge*

The discovery of the form within emptiness and the emptiness within form does not negate the *is*ness of things or the world of appearances. The full moon *is* the full moon; a dream *is* a dream; pain and happiness *are* what they are. Rather the appreciation of emptiness is the realization of things in their

100

own right, in their own nature. The process of uncovering this openness within experience depends on the development of a way of being and seeing that is rooted in the unborn emptiness of the feminine—resting the mind, too, in its own nature.

One cannot experience the emptiness of concepts, or see the world in a direct way, without a discipline, a deliberate practice or approach to experience that encourages one to view oneself and one's world without fear, remorse, or preconceptions. In order to recognize the openness of things, one must first acknowledge the closed world of preconceptions in which one is immersed. The acceptance of discipline in one's life then becomes a willingness to unlearn what one has learned, a willingness to realize the illusoriness and confusion of many of one's ideas and values.

The characteristics of discipline or practice have been recorded in legend as heroic journeys of descent and emergence. Although discipline is conventionally associated with order and method, in its initial stages it is actually characterized by submersion into chaos and confusion. This is symbolized by the descent into Hades of Ulysses and Persephone, by Jonah's sojourn in the belly of the whale, and by the story of the Polynesian Maui, who upon returning from his adventures was made to enter the mouth of his grandmother, the Great Lady of the Night, Hine-nui-te-po. Although these examples are mythical, they highlight actual life situations in which one attempts to confront or suspend preconceptions and to sharpen one's awareness. If you are driving down a hill and your brakes give out, you cannot afford to think about how much this is going to cost or fantasize about the kind of accident you are going to have.

The meaning of discipline as a deliberate effort to exercise and focus one's mind begins with the apparent experience of increased confusion; one discovers the chaos that resides in the darkness of the mind, where one had earlier feared to look. The beginning is the exploration of that darkness, with no expectation of the light that may lie beyond.

The initiation of the shaman and the revelation of the mystic are other forms of entry into the chaotic womb of the unknown. These are often ordeals involving prolonged periods of sickness, fasting, and isolation, punctuated by an intense physical trial that culminates in ecstatic vision. The great revelatory experiences of Moses and Mohammed, Joan of Arc and St. Teresa of Avila, inspired these visionaries with unshakable conviction and the ability to live their visions.

Among the Eskimo this mystical death and rebirth ends when the initiate experiences the illuminating flash of light—*quamaneq*—allowing the future shaman to see clearly into the nature of things. The intensity of the chaos may begin when the Eskimo enters a trance lasting several days within the womblike igloo, during which he envisions himself being swallowed by a giant bear, beast, or animal. This is often followed by a visit from a visionary spirit. The initiatory chaos may even be brought on by actually plunging beneath the ice into the arctic waters and reemerging hours later from another hole in the ice several miles away. These spectacular examples have some

87. Olmec Jaguar priest holding Jaguar baby, who represents emergence of the initiate from the womb of chaos.

101

parallels in the characteristics of psychotic or schizophrenic experience, which is often accompanied by visionary states, but which generally leads to psychic disintegration rather than emergence or spiritual rebirth.

Ecstatic emergence from chaos may lead to a life of inspired works, particularly if the goals or values of a community reinforce the validity of such experience. This has been the sustaining power of many traditional societies. The visions acquired in the chaotic descent may also be used to create dynamic new social values. The growth and power of Islamic civilization is derived from the inspired visions of Mohammed. In a similar way, Christianity and Hinduism repeatedly have renewed themselves through the inspired revelations of their greatest saints and contemplative thinkers, including such contemporaries as Thomas Merton and Ramana Maharshi. The development of American democracy is itself grounded in the vision of the "founding fathers," which was forged during the chaotic descent of the American Revolution. Despite the conviction of the holders of these visions, values based on visionary experience, like the experience itself, are subject to the same laws of impermanence and decay as govern all other natural phenomena. The unceasing motion of the universe swirls and tumbles, here destroying, here creating, all a vast churning in the womb of space. If vision is not continually renewed, it perishes with the turning of the wheel of time.

The whole panorama of the phenomenal world in its infinite variety of forms, each in different stages of coming into and going out of existence, appears very solid. Yet, time and again when we encounter something or someone that we feel very sure about, we discover that our confidence or perception had no practical foundation in reality. Impermanence is a universal expression of the unceasingness of the feminine. Like the moon in its play of fullness and emptiness, like the womb, now vacant, now swollen and heavy with life, the changeableness of the world points beyond itself to an unconditioned ground or matrix.

Having discovered the impermanent nature of experience and having begun to explore the chaos of our lives, the journey is not at all ended, but takes on a quality of greater awareness. The continued descent and reemergence depend on the application of deliberate discipline, conscious attention to the fluctuating world of form and emptiness, reality and dream. In many spiritual traditions, the practice of meditation has been developed to provide this ongoing attention to one's life. Meditation exemplifies a profoundly introspective initiation providing entry into the unborn, unconditioned space that gives birth to clarity of mind.

The practice of meditation begins with a giving up of any expectation, instant gratification, or reward. It depends on the willingness to simply pay attention to or be mindful of one's situation, one's internal and external surroundings. By acknowledging that one is doing nothing more than being mindful, the space is created to see and experience the habitual patterns of thought, feeling, and action, and the possibility arises for more inspired and intelligent action. Initially thoughts and emotions rampage through space,

88. *The Great Red Dragon and the Woman Clothed with the Sun.*
William Blake.

like a river gone wild, overflowing its banks and rushing downstream in the manner of a flash flood. At the same time, one may begin to sense a much larger space that encompasses the chaotic, claustrophobic flow of thoughts, emotions, hopes, and doubts.

> *If the heart wanders or is distracted, bring it back to the point gently and replace it tenderly into its Master's presence. And even if you did nothing during the whole of your hour but bring your heart back and place it again in our Lord's presence, though it went away every time you brought it back, your hour would be very well employed.*
> St. Francis de Sales

Meditation, as a surrender to both chaos and space, neither trying to conquer the mind nor to let go entirely, is the feminine in oneself getting to know itself. This parthenogenic quality or self-fertilization of the feminine occurs when the inherent wisdom and space of the mind become impregnated by and give birth to the clarity and compassionate activity of the masculine. The feminine, in becoming itself through the simple application of attention, also engenders its masculine counterpart.

There are many practices that evoke different states of mental concentration, absorption, visionary exaltation, or profound cosmic abstraction, which are called meditation or contemplation. As the unfiltered and unhindered experience of impermanence, meditation has as its continuing thread or substratum the realization of emptiness, pure space, or the utter poverty of God. From this point of view, meditation is neither an escape nor a means of achieving ecstasy. The liberation that one seeks on the path of meditation is the liberation from confusion, not the unqualified liberation or escape from what one finds unpleasant or undesirable. Experientially, there is a difference between using a contemplative practice to obtain a desirable state of mind or form of existence and cultivating emptiness in order to see things as they are.

Throughout history and myth, the hero's journey through darkness into light has been a transformative passage from confusion to clarity. Clarity or vision depends not on one's wishes but on the unconditioned and unborn nature of existence, the ground of the feminine. Meditation as the disciplined practice of this vision is not the manufacturing of what we desire, but the acknowledgment of what we are.

CHAPTER EIGHT
The Open Journey

THE DESCRIPTION of human experience and relationship in terms of feminine and masculine principles raises basic questions about the nature of our existence, perception, and reality. Feminine and masculine are psychological and cosmic energies inherent in each of us. What does this mean and how does it pertain to us as flesh and blood creatures of a particular sex? Since feminine and masculine are simultaneously existing complementary energies, masculine cannot be equated simply with male and feminine with female.

Ascribing the feminine to space and masculine to personal response and activity does not mean that feminine begins where masculine ends and vice versa. There is an interplay that is so mutually dependent that to try to separate masculine and feminine into two neat categories is impossible. Emotional response could not exist without the psychological and environmental space in which it finds its expression. Approaching feminine and masculine with this understanding in no way undermines, but enhances and enriches respect for one's own manhood or womanhood.

There is no denying that many of the descriptions and qualities that we attribute to the feminine are derived from sexual differentiation and social roles. To explore feminine and masculine qualities without touching upon some of our most fundamental life experiences would be self-deceptive. The personal experiences of every individual are characterized by innumerable differences, points of uniqueness that are there to be appreciated and respected. Yet if feminine and masculine just referred to our social and biological distinctions, this would mean that women and men represent two irreducible opposites. To believe that we as men and women are the manifestations of two absolute poles of experience goes to the roots of chauvinism. A basic aspect of chauvinism is the value and emphasis that has been placed upon the sexual distinctions derived from childbearing. The belief that these distinctions represent the crowning difference in human experience has been institutionalized in many ways and has provided or supported many taboos and social prejudices: witch burnings, face veils, chastity belts, coerced segregation during menstruation, and the legal, moral, and social questions about pornography and prostitution. Anxiety and confusion about our sexuality and passions are so pervasive that it has been difficult to come to terms with and recognize the different ways in which we have supported these beliefs and customs. Ascribing some kind of permanent or absolute difference to our

90. Nyoirin-Kannon, Bodhisattva of Compassion. Japan, 10th century.

experience as either male or female tends to solidify the way we think about ourselves and the world, and therefore communication becomes problematic. To believe that one possesses a particular characteristic—such as a menstrual cycle—that gives one a more profound connection with and intuitive insight into the nature of reality than a man could ever possibly have, creates a fundamental stumbling block to openness.

91. Head of St. John the Baptist, Chartres, 13th century.

Perhaps over all there is a great motherhood, as a common longing. . . . And even in the man there is motherhood, it seems to me, physical and spiritual; his procreating is also a kind of giving birth, and giving birth it is when he creates out of inmost fullness.

R. M. Rilke

We are all the same and we are all different. We all have to face the reality of our birth and death, and of our having to grow up and actualize ourselves while still coping with the world of impermanence. Yet within this shared universal situation we as male and female are unquestionably unique. But the different approaches and experiences of the world that each one of us has are not dependent solely upon sexual distinction. To feel that one characteristic, whether it is sexual, intellectual, or physical, defines who one is, will always induce defensiveness and self-protectiveness. To derive a permanent sense of identity from any of the qualities or energies of experience, whether sexual, emotional, physical, or intellectual, prevents one from seeing the passing nuances of the moment, and mutes appreciation of the relativity of phenomena. To appreciate, to be able to taste and savor a particular experience, a conversation, or a glass of wine, requires an openness and emptiness of preconceptions. The inseparability of emptiness and appreciative warmth returns us to the immediate and transcendent play of feminine and masculine.

108

92.

As a man or a woman each one of us may wish to actualize and refine feminine and masculine qualities with the awareness that one should not be expressed to the detriment of the other. In the healthy interplay of these inseparable energies neither can dilute nor repress the other. As complementary aspects of a whole, feminine and masculine maintain their integrity by each allowing the other its complete expression. The fullness of the one depends upon the openness of the other. Health or sanity is not a half and half proposition but a fearlessness that allows either one of these energies its full manifestation.

109

If one feels that one's style of behavior has a strong feminine quality, this does not necessarily mean that the masculine energy has been conquered or smothered. Perhaps one finds it very easy and natural to act with the accommodating spaciousness of the feminine: to introduce people and to create the easy and generous environment for them to relax and to get to know each other. In this open and gracious way, there may seem to be nothing which is overtly masculine, nothing that one could point to that is equal in vision and intensity to the feminine quality that is being manifest as hosting. However, if the occasion is a success, it is equally due to the gracious counterpoint of the masculine, which allows the feminine its full expression and subtlely lends its clarity to skillfully articulate the situation.

The issue of androgyny is naturally raised whenever feminine and masculine are described as self-existing within each of us. Although there is nothing particularly revolutionary about androgyny, the approach to it may become problematic. By reacting to patriarchal and matriarchal roles, a fear and a misunderstanding may develop about the meaning of the full expression of feminine and masculine. The millennia-old solidity of the identification of male with masculine and female with feminine, compounded by the inheritance of the biases of a powerfully patriarchal social situation, have tended to produce the reactionary idea of androgyny as the creation of a homogenized stasis or equalization of feminine and masculine. In this approach there is a tendency to gloss over the reality of our individual as well as our sexual uniqueness.

Because of the historical polarization of male and female roles, the feminine has often been narrowly stereotyped as an intuitive, emotional, and subservient woman, and the masculine as a selfishly logical, domineering man. In light of these popular views there is a desire to equalize or even to reverse accepted social roles, rather than to try to understand and appreciate the actuality of what we are. Some might argue that because women are essentially feminine, and therefore supposedly more compassionate and less aggressive than men, society would be better off as a matriarchy. The patriarchal logic that women are essentially domestic and belong in the home is the chauvinistic counterpart to the matriarchal logic that women are better fit to run the world. Both of these attitudes have a common foundation: that women hold a copyright on the feminine and men on the masculine. These chauvinist approaches support a mutual warfare, where two combating armies, each with its own territorial imperatives, struggle for beliefs in unqualified specialness.

The contemporary desire to equalize male and female roles is both a reaction to chauvinism and a manifestation of the popular interpretation of androgyny. A common view of androgyny, which holds that each of us is as much male as female, lies behind the concept of unisex. According to this approach, our essential androgyny points to our fundamentally indefinable nature and also to the possibility of transcending sexual differentiation and any role distinctions. The ideal condition is believed to be the balancing of

110

male and female, masculine and feminine, so that the traditional and stereotypical distinctions are dissolved. Whatever kind of androgynous existence this might prove to be, its roots lie in the fear of actualizing what feminine and masculine are, because of their identification with patriarchal and matriarchal roles.

Androgyny has been used as a catchword for human liberation. It is evoked to support women's liberation, homosexuality, bisexuality, transexuality, and transvestitism, or any other breakdown of rigid sexual roles. As an expression of the accumulation of frustrated impulses and repressed values, the popular attitude toward androgyny is epitomized in an anonymous story. Once upon a time there was an isle of detention, called the Prison of Gender. The women were, and always had been, the captive laborers breaking rocks in the sweltering sun, while the men had been confined to the role of giving orders and guarding the women with their guns. One day one of the women said, "Wait a minute! I'm tired of breaking rocks. I want to hold a gun and give orders!" After a certain amount of consternation caused by this outburst, it was finally decided to change roles. But before too long someone else, no one knows for sure who, cried out, "To hell with this! Let's break out of this scene altogether!"

We are confronted with a doublebind: so long as one remains unaware of the potentiality and nondual nature of feminine and masculine and continues to identify them solely with female and male, one will be fearful or even disrespectful of sexual differentiation and incapable of fulfilling one's capacities as a man or a woman. Viewing feminine and masculine as universal and psychological terms rather than strictly sexual ones returns us to a more traditional understanding of and approach to androgyny. Androgyny provides the working basis for the culminating symbol of alchemy: the chemical marriage or the sacred marriage—*hieros-gamos*—the union of feminine and masculine within oneself. In alchemy, feminine and masculine, symbolized by quicksilver and sulpher, moon and sun, are the essential energies to be developed within the individual and nature. Like gold that has to be extracted from the earth, hammered and wrought into shape, feminine and masculine are to be tamed and transmuted before the sacred marriage can occur. Through the sacred marriage the different tensions within the individual are recognized, and consciousness or spirit is slowly purified and merges into a divine knowledge of the whole of nature. The sacred marriage is not the homogenization of feminine and masculine within one, but the recognition and utilization of these complementary energies for the development of an individual to his or her fullest potential.

The refining, transmuting, and marriage of the feminine and masculine within oneself refer to the process of confronting and playing with confusion and passion. The situation of relating to ignorance and confused desire as a direct means of developing a transcendent and precise intelligence, a nonaggressive passion, and an unshakable and dignified way of acting in the world has been beautifully described by a Sufi dervish:

93. Martha Graham.

But the whole purpose of . . . the Way of the dervish, is to give him an escape from this prison, an apocalypse of the Seventy Thousand Veils, a recovery of the original unity with The One, while still in this body. The body is not to be put off; it is to be refined and made spiritual —a help and not a hindrance to the spirit. It is like a metal that has to be refined by fire and transmuted. And the sheikh tells the aspirant that he has the secret of this transmutation. "We shall throw you into the fire of Spiritual Passion," he says, "and you will emerge refined."

Buddhist meditation practice has similarly been described as a gold refinery, whose artistically worked products are perceptive intelligence, *prajna*, and skillful means, *upaya*. Intelligence and skillful behavior relate to each other in a playful give and take, much in the same way as feminine and masculine. Rooted in the openness and intelligence of the feminine, the masculine aspect of mind arises: clarity of insight and compassionate activity. Like a mother imbuing its child with encouragment and love, intelligence and unborn space pervade activity. The more penetrating the insight, the less calculating, more open, and spontaneous, action becomes. Activity soaked with openness becomes a compassionate attitude in which intelligence can function and develop even further.

The inseparable and mutually responding energies of openness and compassionate behavior are the fundamental play of feminine and masculine. Experiencing the attributes of feminine and masculine independent of biological inheritance and associated roles is a shift of dramatic proportions. Feminine and masculine are fundamentally intimate and cosmic expressions of a territoriless reality that is essentially nondual, a oneness or unity, having the expression of two. From this point of view, the world is no longer an extension of one's identifications and expectations, but is something which one can actually relate to, play with, and see as it is.

The universal, personal, and nondual qualities of feminine and masculine were totally interwoven into the androgynous world-view of the European alchemists. As the *Anima Mundi*, the feminine was considered to be the moving spirit of the world connecting and inspiring all the various levels of experience of the universe. The feminine was also identified with the *prima materia*, the primal chaotic and undifferentiated condition of all of the elements comprising the physical world and the realm of the mind.

In the eighteenth century alchemy came to be considered heretical and preposterous by the new European scientific orthodoxy. Replacing God, Reason became the ultimate principle and judge of a now secularized monotheism. Paradoxically, consciousness and the whole realm of the mind were thought to be not only distinct from matter and the phenomenal universe, but an intangible and suspect area of study. The idea of the feminine as an integral part of nature was thought absurd and beneath the consideration of the rational intellect. The banishment of alchemy and its related arts from the laboratories and halls of academia sealed tight the doors leading to the reputable or official recognition of the wisdom of the feminine and an androgynous or nondual point of view. The secularization of religion, in general, and the growing rationalist skepticism of spiritual values added further fuel to the development of the feminine dominion as the black market of the imagination.

With the European lineages of wisdom broken and scattered, the Romantic vision became the illegitimate heir of the deposed realm of the mind. Deprived of its spiritual and psychological disciplines, the mind nurtured itself on dreams and fantasies.

94. *Starry Vault of the Queen of Night*. Karl Friedrich Schinkel.

The Night became the mighty womb of revelations.

Novalis

Within its primal home, the womb of night, the feminine gave birth to the modern traditions of aesthetic and cultural revolution, as well as to the development of psychotherapy. As the child of darkness, the dream was cultivated by the European Romantic poets and artists who found in it the inspiration to offset a life bereft of spiritual value. It was Sigmund Freud, however, who brought the significance of the dream and the unconscious to the attention of the mainstream of society. In his pioneering psychoanalytic work, Freud perceived the intimate relationship of the seemingly contradictory drives toward love and death, *eros* and *thanatos*. Focusing on these two forces, he had actually presented a psychological description of two of the most

114

powerful qualities that had once been attributed to the Great Mother. The question of why the forces of love and death should appear to arouse such fear provided Freud with the major impetus for his life work.

> *Time and Space are Real Beings, a Male and a Female. Time is a Man, Space is a Woman, and her Masculine Portion is Death.*
>
> Geza Roheim

In his final book, *Civilization and its Discontents,* Freud maintained that civilization can only exist through the repression of these basic instinctual drives. Precisely because of this, Freud felt that civilization was doomed. According to Freud, prolonged repression results in the enervation of civilization's intrinsic vitality, while at the same time promoting and encouraging hostility in its own ranks. Being fundamentally of the rationalist persuasion, Freud's analysis of the double-bind situation of civilization is mirror perfect. His pessimistic conclusions are understandable in light of his acceptance of masculine superiority and his belief that the cultivation of feminine qualities are a dangerous and major contributing factor to neurosis.

95. *Vampire.*
Edvard Munch.

THE FEMININE   Freud's mistrust of the feminine was furthered by a lack of any traditional context in which to work with and integrate the feminine. His pupil Carl G. Jung, in attempting to reestablish a relationship with alchemy, discovered the feminine as a vital and necessary regenerative force. While reaffirming the ideal of androgyny, he also developed the concepts of *anima* and *animus*. Jung believed the *anima* to be the compensatory feminine in relation to the dominant masculine in the male, and the *animus* to be the compensatory masculine in relation to the dominant feminine in the female. Although the *anima* and *animus* theory continues to uphold sexual polarization, a central theme of Jung's therapeutic approach was to reintroduce the feminine into the essentially masculine, patriarchically dominated ego. According to the Jungian approach, if the problems we experience are due to the repressive and crippling effects of the masculine ego, then

> *the end of analysis coincides with the acceptance of femininity.*
> James Hillman, *The Myth of Analysis*

Psychoanalysis and the contemporary therapeutic movement are vital functions of a culture dominated by masculine values. Whatever the ideology of a given therapy, it has to relate to the insidious pervasiveness of male dominance that is interwoven with and buttressed by the exaggerated masculine attributes of aggressiveness, competitiveness, and mistrust of the body and the emotions. In working with the imbalance of civilization, the contemporary therapeutic movements generally point toward a holistic affirmation of the individual.

The challenge today is to live with dignity and sanity in the face of chaos. This is a personal responsibility that depends upon a recognition and appreciation of one's essential aloneness. Through renouncing one's idealistic attachments, as well as the desire to be a particular kind of person, one opens oneself to a humility and an emptiness that can enrich the quality of experience. This may mean an owning up to the fact that one does not have all the answers, and perhaps even a surrendering of the answers one believes one already has. In this way each situation can present itself as new and unique.

Seeing everything and everyone as having the essential spacious and open nature of the unborn feminine, one may experience the whole of creation as one's mother. Allowing oneself to be in the basic condition of aloneness, space begins to eat away at one's basic doubts and fears. Through continual exposure to boundless space, the obscurities that keep one from seeing clearly may slowly be cleaned away, much the way a mother changes a baby's diapers, bathes it, and keeps its nose clean. As the elements of ignorance and habitual thought become corroded by space, one begins to discover a basic confidence and fearlessness that have nothing to do with asserting a particular idea, but that simply arise out of the unhindered experience of empty space. Like the primordial Great Mother, the vastness of space and mind is continually accommodating and devouring thoughts, feelings, and emotions.

96. Dancing Apsaras. Cambodia.

Confidence must precede all things like a mother her child.
It guards and increases all positive things.
It removes fears and rescues from the rivers of pain and suffering.
Confidence is the road sign to the citadel of happiness.

                              Ratnōlkānamadhārani

THE FEMININE   The qualities of fearlessness and openness, masculine and feminine, are reciprocal. Not afraid of making a fool of oneself, and trusting the intelligence inseparable from openness, one could enter a situation with a sense of pleasure and a lack of regret. With one's confidence rooted in the expansiveness and intelligence of unborn space, the mind can relax, and its original clarity and openness can emerge. Imbued with generosity and compassion toward oneself and the world, one can then act precisely, no longer holding to any reference point—the only guideline being the spontaneous play of the phenomenal world. Not being confined by prejudices or ideals about feminine and masculine, one can begin to see them as fundamental expressions of who one is and how one creates the world in which we live.

The union of feminine and masculine as the inseparability of discriminating awareness and skillful compassionate behavior could be developed as a life-embracing discipline. As the basic aspects of a way in which one might work with the energy of the world intelligently and compassionately, feminine and masculine point to a journey that, being rooted in the unborn, is without end. Living a life with no ultimate resting point may seem to be impossible or even undesirable. Yet it is precisely the hopes and fears aroused by holding onto a particular reference point that cloud one's perceptions of things as they are and separate one from the world. This feeling of being simultaneously fearful and estranged feeds the potential for conflict, aggression, and chauvinism. As men and women, a life of dignity, free from attachment to any particular ideology or concept of what one might be, arises from accepting confusion as the working base for discovering greater warmth and intelligence. The marriage of feminine and masculine, openness and compassion, is an ongoing path leading to fresh experience, spontaneous humor, and an alert intelligence.

The spirit of the valley never dies.
This is called the mysterious female.
The gateway of the mysterious female
Is called the root of heaven and earth.
Dimly visible, it seems as it were scarcely there,
Yet use will never drain it.

Lao Tzu

97. Calligraphy. Chögyam Trungpa, Rinpoche.

98.

Anthology

THIS BRIEF ANTHOLOGY is intended to convey and evoke in the words and language of diverse traditions and thinkers the universal qualities of the feminine. The placement of the selections is designed to accompany and embellish the flow of the text.

There is something in the soul which is uncreated and uncreatable.

Meister Eckhardt

There is an Unborn, Unbecome, Unmade, Uncompounded; for if there were not this Unborn, Unbecome, Unmade, Uncompounded, there would be apparently no escape from this *here* that is born, become, made, and compounded.

Buddha

From the nothing the begetting:
from the nothing the abundance:
the power of increasing, the living breath:
it dwelt within the empty space
it produced the firmament which is above us.

Maori cosmology

Before the Beginning of things Thou didst exist in the form of Tamas which is beyond both speech and mind, and of Thee by the creative desire of the Supreme Brahman was the universe born. . . .

Because Thou devourest Kala (time), Thou art Kali, because Thou art the Origin of and devourest all things Thou art called the Adya Kali. Resuming after dissolution Thine own nature, dark and formless, ineffable and inconceivable Thou alone remainest as the One. Though having a form yet art Thou formless; though Thyself without beginning, multiform by the power of Maya, Thou art Beginning of all, creatrix, protectress, and destructress that Thou art. Hence it is O gentle One!

Hymn to Kali

I am she that is the natural mother of all things, mistress and governess of all the elements, the initial progeny of worlds, chief of the powers divine, queen of all that are in hell, the principal of those that dwell in heaven, manifested alone and under one form of all the gods and goddesses. At my will the planets of the sky, the wholesome winds of the seas, and the lamentable silences of hell are disposed; my name, my divinity is adored throughout the world, in diverse manners in variable customs, and by many names.

Lucius Apuleius

THE FEMININE   I will sing of well-founded earth, mother of all, eldest of beings. She feeds all creatures that are in the world, all that go upon the goodly land, and all that are in the paths of the seas and all that fly: all these are fed of her store. Through you O queen, men are blessed in their children and blessed in their harvests, and to you it belongs to give means of life to mortal men and to take it away . . . .

Hail, Mother of the gods, wife of starry heaven; freely bestow upon me for this my song substance that cheers the heart! And now I will remember you and another song also!

Homeric hymn

Empress of the highest,
Mistress over the lowest,
Chosen path of Heaven,
Held fast by faithful hope,
Those separated from you far,
Recalled to you, unite
In your fold!

Adam de Saint Victor

At the threshold of the ninth dwelling
—O inconceivable mystery,
must I reveal to you
the Mother of mothers
the majestic, eternal Mother?

Lalan Fakir

The Receptive brings about sublime success,
Furthering through the perseverance of a mare.
If the superior man undertakes something and tries to lead,
He goes astray;
But if he follows, he finds guidance. . . .

Perfect indeed is the sublimity of the Receptive. All beings owe their birth to it, because it receives the heavenly with devotion.

The Receptive in its riches carries all things. Its nature is in harmony with the boundless. It embraces everything in its breadth and illumines everything in its greatness. Through it all individual beings attain success.

I Ching

Know that when you learn to lose yourself, you will reach the Beloved. There is no other secret to be learnt, and more than this is not known to me.

Ansari of Herat

Virgin Mother, daughter of thy son, lowly and uplifted more than any creature, fixed
    goal of the eternal counsel,
Thou art she who didst human nature so ennoble that its own Maker scorned not to
    become its making.

122

In thy womb was lit again the love under whose warmth in the eternal peace this
    flower hath thus unfolded.
Here art thou unto us the meridian torch of love and here below with mortals art a
    living spring of hope.

Dante

The sect of lovers is distinct from all others;
Lovers have a religion and a faith all their own.

Jalal-uddin-Rumi

The world had a beginning
And this beginning could be called the mother of the world.
When you know the mother
Go on to know the child.
After you have known the child
Go back to holding fast to the mother,
And to the end of your days you will not meet with danger.

Lao Tzu

First of all the Emptiness came into being, next broad-bosomed earth, the solid and
eternal home of all, and Desire, the most beautiful of the immortal gods. . . . Out of
Emptiness came Darkness and black Night, and out of Night came Light and Day, her
children conceived after union in love with Darkness.

Hesiod

This they are coming to see!
I am going to make a place which is sacred.
This they are coming to see.
White Buffalo Cow Woman Appears
Is sitting in a *wakan* manner.
They are all coming to see her!

These peoples are sacred;
From all over the universe they are coming to see it.
White Buffalo Cow Woman Appears is sitting here in a sacred manner;
They are all coming to see her.

Black Elk

Of old, Heaven and Earth were not yet separated and the In and Yo not yet divided.
They formed a chaotic mass like an egg which was of obscurely defined limits and
contained germs. . . .

The Nihongi Chronicles

The Egg broke open. The two halves were, one of silver, the other of gold. The silver
one became the earth, the golden one the sky; the thick membrane (the yolk) became

the mist with the clouds, the small veins the rivers, the fluid the sea. And what was born from it was the Sun.

Chandogya Upanishad

The lower half of the egg shall be the roof of the earth;
The upper part of the egg shall become the high sky.
Whatever is white in the egg shall beam sweetly as the moon.
The other parts of the egg shall become the stars of heaven.

Kalevala

Maya makes all things: what moves, what is unmoving.
O son of Kunti, that is why the world spins,
Turning its wheel through birth
And through Destruction.

Bhagavad Gita

Bhikkhus, there are four incalculables of the aeon. What four? The contraction, what supercedes the contraction, the expansion, and what supercedes the expansion.

Buddha

What of the future? Will the universe expand forever to a final state where no further energy is available, or will it recreate itself by collapsing again to a singular condition of infinite density? We do not know the answer. We do not know whether the expansion is solely the result of the initial motion of the particles at the beginning of time or whether the expansion is determined by a cosmological force of repulsion—a force opposing gravitational attraction which appears as a consequence of some solutions of the equations of general relativity. Hence we do not know whether the universe contains enough matter to overcome by gravitational attraction the forces now driving the galaxies apart. There are some who are willing to interpret the present data about the deceleration of the distant galaxies as an indication that the universe will collapse, and that it is forever cyclical, successively evolving and collapsing to the singular state of infinite density. In this case we may be privileged to exist in a unique cycle of the total history of the cosmos where the delicacy of the balance of the constants of nature narrowly determined the possibility that a part, at least, of this cycle should be knowable. . . . Human existence is itself entwined with the primeval state of the universe, and the pursuit of understanding is a transcendent value in man's life and purpose.

Sir Bernard Lovell

Now when a Bhikkhu capable of recollecting aeons is recollecting his former life, then of such aeons as these he recollects *many aeons of world contraction, many aeons of world expansion, many aeons of world contraction and expansion.*

Buddhagosa

And the Lord God said, Behold, the man is become as one of us, to know good and evil: and now, lest he put forth his hand and take also of the tree of life, and eat and live forever:

124

Therefore the Lord God sent him forth from the Garden of Eden, to till the ground from whence he was taken.

So he drove out the man; and he placed at the east of the Garden of Eden Cherubims, and a flaming sword which turned every way, to keep the way of the tree of life.

Genesis

Then Gilgamesh opened his mouth again and said to Enkidu, "My friend, let us go to the Great Palace, to Egalmah, and stand before Ninsun the Queen. Ninsun is wise with deep knowledge, she will give us counsel for the road we must go." They took each other by the hand as they went to Egalmah, and they went to Ninsun the great Queen. Gilgamesh approached, he entered the palace and spoke to Ninsun. "Ninsun, will you listen to me; I have a long journey to go, to the land of Humbaba, I must travel an unknown road and fight a strange battle. From the day I go until I return, til I reach the cedar forest and destroy the evil which Shamash abhors, pray for me to Shamash."

Ninsun went into her room, she put on a dress becoming to her beautiful body, she put on jewels to make her breast beautiful, she placed a tiara on her head and her skirts swept the ground. Then she went up to the altar of the Sun, standing upon the roof of the palace; she burnt incense and lifted her arms to Shamash as the smoke ascended: "O Shamash, why did you give this restless heart to Gilgamesh, my son; why did you give it? You have moved him and now he sets out on a long journey to the land of Humbaba, to travel an unknown road and to fight a strange battle. Therefore from the day that he goes til the day he returns, until he reaches the cedar forest, until he kills Humbaba and destroys the evil thing which you, Shamash, abhor, do not forget him; but let the dawn, Aya your dear bride, remind you always, and when day is done give him to the watchman of the night to keep him from harm." Then Ninsun the mother of Gilgamesh extinguished the incense, and she called to Enkidu with this exhortation: "Strong Enkidu, you are not the child of my body, but I will receive you as my adopted son; you are my other child like the foundlings they bring to the temple. Serve Gilgamesh as a foundling serves the temple and the priestess who reared him. In the presence of my women, my votaries and hierophants, I declare it." Then she placed the amulet for a pledge round his neck, and she said to him, "I entrust my son to you; bring him back to me safely."

Epic of Gilgamesh

As long as the world exists
It manifests in various ways
Seeking birth
In the impure realms,
Entering a womb and being born,
Being versed in art,
Amused by the company of women,
Leaving home, practicing austerities
Sitting under the Bodhi-tree,
Conquering the armies of Mara
Turning the Dharmachakra of enlightenment and
Passing into Nirvana.

Uttaratantra

THE FEMININE The mother of our songs, the mother of all our seed, bore us in the beginning of things and so she is the mother of all types of men, the mother of all nations. She is the mother of the thunder, the mother of the streams, the mother of trees and of all things. She is the mother of the world and of the older brothers, the stone-people. She is the mother of the fruits of the earth and of all things. She is the mother of our younger brothers, the French, and the strangers. She is the mother of our dance paraphernalia, of all of our temples, and she is the only mother we possess. She alone is the mother of the fire and the Sun and the Milky Way. . . . She is the mother of the rain and the only mother we possess. And she has left us a token in all the temples, a token in the form of songs and dances.

Whose seeds are we? To our mother alone do we belong.

Myth of Creation of Kagaba People

Then even nothingness was not, nor existence.
There was no air, nor the heavens beyond it.
What covered? Where was it? In whose keeping?
Was there then cosmic water in depths unfathomed?
Then there were neither death nor immortality.
Nor was there then the torch of night and day.
The One breathed windlessly and self-sustaining.
There was that One then, and there was no Other.
At first there was only darkness wrapped in darkness.
All this was only unillumined water.
That One which came to be, enclosed in nothing,
arose at last, born of the power of heat.
In the beginning desire descended on it—
that was the primal seed, born of the mind.
The sages who looked into their hearts with wisdom
know that is, is kin to that which is not.
And they have stretched their cord across the void,
And know what was above and what below.
Seminal powers made fertile mighty forces.
Below was strength and over it was impulse.
But, after all, who knows and who can say
when it all came, and how creation happened?
The gods themselves are later than creation,
so who knows truly when it arose?
When all creation had its origin,
he, whether he fashioned it or whether he did not,
he who surveys it all from highest heaven,
he knows—or maybe even he does not know.

Rig Veda

In primitive times people dwelt in caves and lived in forests. The holy men of a later time made the change to buildings. At the top was a ridgepole, and sloping down from it there was a roof, to keep off wind and rain. . . .

I Ching

126

The men of old, while the chaotic condition was yet undeveloped, shared the placid tranquility which belonged to the whole world. At that time the Yin and Yang were harmonious and still; their resting and movement proceeded without any disturbance; the four seasons had their definite times; not a single thing received any injury, and no living being came to a premature end. Men might be possessed of the faculty of knowledge, but they had no occasion for its use. This was what is called the state of Perfect Unity. At this time, there was no action on the part of any one, but a constant manifestation of spontaneity.

This condition of excellence deteriorated and decayed. . . . After this they forsook their nature and followed the promptings of their minds. One mind and another associated their knowledge, but were unable to give rest to the world. Then they added to this knowledge external and elegant forms, and went on to make these more and more numerous. The forms extinguished the primal simplicity, til the mind was drowned by their multiplicity. After this the people began to be perplexed and disordered, and had no way by which they might return to their true nature and bring back their original condition.

Chuang Tzu

The ancients who preserved the Way in their own persons did not try by sophistical reasonings to gloss over their knowledge; they did not seek to embrace everything in the world in their knowledge, nor to comprehend all the virtues in it. Solitary and trembling they remained where they were, and sought the restoration of their nature. What had they to do with any further action? The Way indeed is not to be pursued, nor all its characteristics to be known on a small scale. A little knowledge is injurious to those characteristics; small doings are injurious to the Way;—hence it is said, "They simply rectified themselves." Complete enjoyment is what is meant by "Attainment of the Aim."

Chuang Tzu

Do men have roots, are they real?
No one can know completely
what is Your richness, what are Your flowers
Oh Inventor of Yourself!
We leave things unfinished,
for this I weep,
I lament.
Here with flowers I interweave my friends.

Let us rejoice!
Our common house is the earth.
In the place of mystery beyond,
is it like this also?
Truly it is not the same.
On earth; flowers and songs
Let us live here!

Nahuatl song

127

THE FEMININE The rout and destruction of the passions, while a good, is not the ultimate good; the discovery of Wisdom is the surpassing good. When this is found, all the people will rejoice.

Philo

Doth not wisdom cry? And understanding put forth her voice?
She standeth in the top of high places, by the way in the places of the paths.
She crieth at the gates, at the entry of the city, at the coming in at the doors.
Unto you, O men, I call; and my voice *is* to the sons of men.
O ye simple, understand wisdom: and ye fools, be ye of an understanding heart.
Hear; for I will speak of excellent things; and the opening of my lips *shall be* of right things.
For my mouth shall speak the truth; and wickedness is an abomination to my lips. . . .
The Lord possessed me in the beginning of his way, before his works of old.
I was set up from everlasting time from the beginning, or ever the earth was.
When *there were* no depths, I was brought forth; when *there were* no fountains abounding with water.
Before the mountains were settled, before the hills was I brought forth:
While as yet he had not made the earth, nor the fields, nor the highest part of the dust of the world.
When he prepared the heavens, I *was* there: when he set a compass upon the face of the deep:
When he established the clouds above: when he strengthened the fountains of the deep:
When he gave to the sea his decree, that the waters should not pass his commandment:
When he appointed the foundations of the earth:
Then I was by him, *as* one brought up *with him*: and I was daily *his* delight, rejoicing always before him;
Rejoicing in the habitable part of his earth: and my delights were with the sons of men.
Now therefore hearken unto me, O ye children: for blessed *are they that* keep my ways.
Hear instruction, and be wise, and refuse it not.
Blessed is the man that heareth me, watching daily at my gates, waiting at the posts of my doors.
For who so findeth me findeth life, and shall obtain favor of the Lord.
But he that sinneth against me wrongeth his own soul: all they that hate me love death.

Proverbs

The monastic Church is the Church of the wilderness, the woman who has fled into the desert from the dragon that seeks to devour the infant Word. She is the Church who, by her silence, nourishes and protects the seed of the Gospel that is sown by the Apostles in the hearts of the faithful. She is the Church who, by her prayer, gains strength for the Apostles themselves, so often harrassed by the monster. The Monastic Church is the one who flees to a special place prepared for her by God in the

wilderness, and hides her face in the Mystery of the divine silence, and prays while
the great battle is being fought between heaven and earth.

Thomas Merton

There is, monks, that sphere wherein there is neither earth nor water nor fire nor air;
there is neither the sphere of infinite space nor of infinite consciousness nor of nothingness nor of the sphere of neither-perception-nor-nonperception; where there is
neither this world nor the world beyond nor both together, nor moon nor sun; this I
say is free from coming and going, from duration and decay; there is no beginning nor
establishment, no result, no cause; this indeed is the end of suffering.

Buddha

Know the male
But keep to the role of the female
And be a valley to the empire.
If you are a valley to the empire,
Then the constant virtue will not desert you
And you will again return to being a babe.

Lao Tzu

O savior Virgin, Star of Sea,
Who bore our child the Son of Justice.
The Source of Light, Virgin always
Hear our praise!

Queen of Heaven who have given
Medicine to the sick, Grace to the devout,
Joy to the sad, Heaven's light to the world
And hope of salvation;

Court royal, Virgin typical,
Grant us cure and guard,

Accept our vows, and by prayers
Drive all griefs away!

Saint Bernard of Clairveaux

All that is hidden, all that is plain, I have come to know
Instructed by Wisdom who designed them all.
For within Her is a spirit intelligent, holy,
Unique, manifold, subtle,
Active, incisive, unsullied,
Lucid, invulnerable, benevolent, sharp,
Irresistible, beneficent, loving to man,
Steadfast, dependable, unperturbed,
Allmighty, all-surveying,
Penetrating all intelligent, pure
And most subtle spirits;
For Wisdom is quicker to move than any motion;
She is so pure, She pervades and permeates all things.

THE FEMININE   She is a breath of the power of God,
Pure emanation of the glory of the Almighty. . . .
She is indeed more splendid than the sun.
She outshines all the constellations:
Compared with light she takes first place,
For light must yield to night, but over Wisdom darkness can never triumph.

Jerusalem Bible

O son of noble family, listen. Now the pure luminosity of the dharmata is shining before you; recognize it. O son of noble family, at this moment your state of mind is by nature pure emptiness, it does not possess any nature whatever, neither substance nor quality such as color, but it is pure emptiness; this is the dharamata, the female Buddha, Samantabhadri. But this state of mind is not just blank emptiness, it is unobstructed sparkling, pure and vibrant; this mind is the male Buddha Samantabhadra. These two, your mind whose nature is emptiness without any substance whatever, and your mind which is vibrant and luminous are inseparable; this is the dharmakaya of the Buddha. This mind of yours is inseparable luminosity and emptiness in the form of a great mass of light, it has no birth or death, therefore it is the Buddha of Immortal Light. To recognize this is all that is necessary. When you recognize this pure nature of your mind as the Buddha, looking into your own mind is resting in the buddhamind.

The Tibetan Book of the Dead

When I was to become a shaman, I chose suffering through the two things that are most dangerous to us humans, suffering through hunger and suffering through cold. . . . My instructor was the husband of my father's wife, Perqaneq . . . he dragged me on a little sledge that was no bigger than I could sit on. . . . It was in wintertime and took place at night with the new moon; it had just appeared in the sky; one could just see the very first streak of the new moon. I was not fetched again until the next moon was of the same size. Perqaneq built a small snow hut no bigger than I could just get under cover and sit down. . . . My novitiate took place in the coldest winter, and I, who never got anything to warm me, and must not move, was very cold, and it was so tiring having to sit without daring to lie down, that sometimes it was as if I died a little. Only towards the end of the thirty days did a helping spirit come to me, a lovely and beautiful helping spirit, whom I had never thought of; it was a white woman; she came to me while I had collapsed, exhausted, and was sleeping. But still I saw her lifelike, hovering over me, and from that day I could not close my eyes or dream without seeing her.

Igjugarjuk, Caribou Eskimo

Liberated from his earthly condition, the ancestor was taken in charge by the regenerating Pair. The male Nummo led him into the depths of the earth, where, in the waters of the womb of his partner he curled himself up like a foetus and shrank to germinal form, and acquired the quality of water, the seed of God and the essence of the two spirits. And all the process was the work of the Word. The male with his voice accompanied the female Nummo who was speaking to herself and to her own sex.

130

The spoken Word entered into her and wound itself round her womb in a spiral of eight turns. Just as the helical band of copper round the sun gives to it its daily movement, so the spiral of the Word gave to the womb its regenerative movement. . . . At the moment of the second instruction, therefore men were living in dens which were already, in some sort, a prefiguration of the place of revelation and of the womb into which each of them in due course would descend to be regenerated.

Ogotemelli, Dogon tribe, Africa

But I concentrate my mind so as to ignore all these contaminations (of ignorance) and return to the mysterious enlightening nature of non-death and non-rebirth so as to be in conformity with the Womb of Tathagata. Accordingly Tathagata's Womb becomes the clear intelligence of the true and mysterious Mind of Intuition that throws its perfect reflection and insight into all the phenomenal world. Therefore, in Tathagata's Womb Oneness has the same meaning as Infinity, and Infinity has the same meaning as Oneness. . . . Nevertheless the Womb of Tathagata is pure and perfect, all embracing but free from distinctions. In it is neither the finite mind, nor empty space, nor the earth, nor water, nor wind, nor fire, nor the senses, nor the whole body, nor sensations, nor perceptions, nor the sphere of consciousness that is dependent on the thinking mind. It is neither the enlightening nature of the Intuitive Mind, nor the non-enlightening nature of the intellectual mind, nor the mental state that discards all ideas relating to enlightenment and non-enlightenment. . . . It is neither Wisdom nor attainment. . . . Nevertheless, if you rightly realize the true meaning of the Tathaga-ta's Womb in its mysterious nature of the natural Enlightening Mind, you will also realize that this mysterious nature is also the thinking mind; empty space; earth, water, wind, and fire; the sense organs, the whole body, sensations, perceptions, discriminations, the sphere of consciousness dependent upon the senses; enlightenment and non-enlightenment; the state that is neither enlightenment nor non-enlightenment; it is the state of decay and death, and the absence of all ideas about decay and death. . . . It is Wisdom, it is all the transcendental attainments. . . . It is Eternity, and Blissful Peace, and ego-consciousness, and Perfect Unity and Purity. And because Tathagata's Essential Mind contains all these it not only conveys the true meaning of Emancipation but of everyday life as well.

Surangama Sutra

Will I have to go like the flowers that perish?
Will nothing remain of my name?
Nothing of my fame here on earth?
At least my flowers, at least my songs!
Earth is the region of the fleeting moment.
Is it also thus in the place
where in some way one lives?
Is there joy there, is there friendship?
Or is it only here on earth
We come to know our faces?

Tecayehuatzin, Aztec

131

THE FEMININE   There is neither creation nor destruction, neither destiny nor free-will.
Neither path nor achievement; this is the final truth.

Ramana Maharshi

Thus in my real nature, vast like celestial space
I have obtained the reality of eternal freedom.

Mahasamvarodayatantraraja

Now the Tao shows itself in two forms; the Pure and the Turbid, and has the two conditions of motion and rest. Heaven is pure and earth is turbid, heaven moves and earth is at rest. The masculine is pure and the feminine is turbid; the masculine moves and the feminine is still.
The radical purity descended and the turbid issue flowed abroad; and thus all things were produced.
The pure is the source of the turbid, and motion is the foundation of rest.
If man could always be pure and still, heaven and earth would both revert to non-existence.
Now the spirit of man loves Purity, but his mind disturbs it. The mind of man loves stillness, but his desires draw it away. If he could always send his desires away, his mind would of itself become still. Let his mind become pure and clean, and his spirit will of itself become pure. . . .
The reason why men are not able to attain to this is because they have not been cleansed, and their desires not sent away. If one is able to send the desires away, when he then looks in at his mind, it is no longer his; and when he looks out at his body, it is no longer his; and when he looks farther off at external things, they are things which he has nothing to do with.
When he understands these three things, there will appear to him only vacancy. This contemplation of vacancy will awaken the idea of vacuity. Without such vacuity there is no vacancy.
The idea of vacuous space having vanished, that of nothingness itself also disappears; and when the idea of nothingness has disappeared, there ensues serenely the condition of constant stillness.

Ching Kang King

Where does your mind seek?
Where is your heart?
If you give your heart to everything,
you lead it nowhere; you destroy your heart.
Can anything be found on earth?

Nahuatl poem

However, the fact that conscious experience can be remembered and therefore must be supposed to be connected with permanent changes in the constitution of the organism points to a comparison between psychical experiences and physical observations. With respect to relationships between conscious experiences we also encounter features reminiscent of the conditions for the comprehension of atomic phenomena. The rich vocabulary used in the communications of the states of our

132

mind refers indeed to a typical complementary mode of description corresponding to a continual change of the content on which attention is focused.

Neils Bohr

No, Mahamati, my Womb of Tathagatahood is not the same as the Divine Atman as taught by the philosophers. What I teach is Tathagatahood in the sense of the Dharmakaya, Ultimate Oneness, Nirvana, emptiness, unbornness, unqualifiedness, devoid of will-effort. The reason why I teach the doctrine of Tathagatahood is to cause the ignorant and simpleminded to lay aside their fears as they listen to the teaching of egolessness and come to understand the state of non-discrimination and imagelessness. . . . The doctrine of the Tathagata-womb is disclosed in order to awaken philosophers from their clinging to the notion of a Divine Atman as a transcendental personality, so that their minds that have become attached to the imaginary notion of "soul" as being something self-existent may be quickly awakened to a state of perfect enlightenment. All such notions as causation, succession, atoms, Supreme Spirit, Sovereign God, Creator, are all figments of the imagination and manifestations of the mind. . . .
Noble Wisdom is a perfect state of imagelessness; it is the Womb of "Suchness"; it is the all-conserving Divine Mind which in its pure Essence forever abides in perfect patience and undisturbed tranquility.

Lankavatara Sutra

A man must become truly poor and free from his own creaturely will as he was when he was born. And I tell you, by the eternal truth, that so long as you *desire* to fulfill the will of God and have any hankering after eternity and God, for just so long you are not truly poor. He alone has true spiritual poverty who wills nothing, knows nothing, desires nothing.

Meister Eckhardt

Thus have I heard: once the Blessed One was dwelling in the royal domain of the Vulture Peak Mountain, together with a great gathering of monks and Bodhisattvas. At that time the Blessed One entered the samadhi which examines the dharmas, called "Profound Illumination," and at the same time noble Avalokiteshvara, the Bodhisattva-Mahasattva, looking at the profound practice of transcendent knowledge, saw the five skandhas and their natural emptiness.

Then through the inspiration of the Buddha, Shariputra said to Avalokiteshvara: "How should those noble ones learn, who wish to follow the profound practice of transcendent knowledge?" And Avalokiteshvara answered: "Shariputra, whoever wishes to follow the profound practice of transcendent knowledge should look at it like this, seeing the five skandhas and their natural emptiness. Form is emptiness, emptiness itself is form; emptiness is no other than form, form is no other than emptiness; in the same way feeling, perception, concept and consciousness are emptiness. Thus all the dharmas are emptiness and have no characteristics. They are unborn and unceasing, they are not impure or pure, they neither decrease nor increase. Therefore since there is emptiness there is no form, no feeling, no perception, no concept, no consciousness; no eye, no ear, no nose, no tongue, no body, no mind; no appearance, no sound, no smell, no taste, no sensation, no objects of mind; no quality of sight, no quality of hearing, no quality of smelling, no quality of tasting, no quality of sensing, no quality of thought, no quality of mind-consciousness; there are no nidanas, from ignorance to old age and death, nor their wearing out; there is no suffering, no cause of suffering, no ending of suffering and no path; no wisdom, no attainment and no non-attainment. Therefore since there is no attainment, the Bodhisattvas abide by means of transcendent knowledge; and since there is no obscurity of mind they have no fear, they transcend falsity and pass beyond the bounds of sorrow. All the Buddhas who dwell in the past, present and future, by means of transcendent knowledge fully and clearly awaken to unsurpassed, true, complete enlightenment. Therefore the mantra of transcendent knowledge, the mantra of deep insight, the unsurpassed mantra, the unequalled mantra, the mantra which calms all suffering should be known as truth, for there is no deception. In transcendent knowledge the mantra is proclaimed:

Om gate gate paragate parasamgate bodhi svaha

O Shariputra, this is how a Bodhisattva-Mahasattva should learn profound transcendent knowledge."

Then the Blessed One arose from that samadhi and praised the Bodhisattva-Mahasattva Avalokiteshvara, saying: "Good, good, O son of noble family! Profound transcendent knowledge should be practiced just as you have taught, and the Tathagatas will rejoice."

When the Blessed One had said this, Shariputra and Avalokiteshvara, that whole gathering and the world with its gods, men, asuras and gandharvas, their hearts full of joy, praised the words of the Blessed One.

Prajnaparamita Hridaya Sutra, The Heart Sutra, or
The Sutra on the Essence of Transcendent Knowledge

Similarly is it with the human soul, which is divided in two—*sechel* (intellect) and *middot* (emotional attributes). The intellect includes chochmah, binah and da'at (ChaBaD), whilst the *middot* are love of G-d, dread and awe of Him, glorification of Him, etc. ChaBaD (the intellectual faculties) are called "mothers" and source of the *middot*, for the latter are "offspring" of the former.

Rabbi S. Z. Zalman of Liadi

It goes beyond the realm of a single world creation myth to an almost universal conception of mankind that the right side is regarded as male and the left as female.

Hermann Baumann

The Great Spirit made our body of two principles, good and evil. The left side is good for it contains the heart. The right side is evil for it has no heart. The left side is awkward but wise. The right side is clever and strong, but it lacks wisdom. There would be a constant struggle between the two sides, and by our actions we would have to decide which was stronger, the evil or the good.

Dan Katchongva, Hopi

I am Atum, the creator of the Eldest Gods,
I am he who gave birth to Shu,
I am that great He-She,
I am he who did what seemed good to him,

I took my space in the place of my will,
Mine is the space of those who move along
like these two serpentine circles.

Egyptian hymn

Mother of the Gods, Father of the Gods,
the Old God,
distended in the navel of the earth,
engaged in the closure of turquoise.

Nahuatl song

. . . for the original human nature was not like the present, but different. The sexes
were not two as they are now but originally three in number; there was man, woman,
and the union of the two, having a name corresponding to this double nature, which
had once a real existence, but is now lost, and the word "Androgynous" is only
preserved as a term of reproach. . . . Zeus cut men in two, like a sorb-apple which is
halved for pickling . . . so ancient is the desire of one another which is implanted in
us, reuniting our original nature, making one of two, and healing the state of man.
Each of us when separated, having one side only, like a flat fish, is but the indenture
of a man and he is always looking for his other half. Men who are a section of that
double nature which was once called Androgynous are lovers of women.

Plato

I. I see the image of a lake. In that lake, there is a man and a woman. They are
holding hands.
II. The man and woman fall into a deep slumber.
III. Through the water, see them embracing each other in a deep sleep.
IV. I see the image of the lake. Standing by the shore at the edge of the lake is a
fisherman. He holds a pole with a net on the end, and scoops it into the sea.
V. He scoops up the woman. She is transformed into a fish, and she is in the net.
VI. The fisherman scoops up the man, who is also transformed into a fish, and he
is in the net.
VII. I see the image of a house or cottage. At the table, the fisherman slices the fish.
The woman has been sliced into fillets or sections. The man, who has become a
fish, is in the process of being sliced.
VIII. I see this being collected and put into a large glass container, which looks like a
crystal coffin. This crystal coffin is sitting by a fireplace.
IX. The fisherman stokes the fire.
X. There is a great flame within the fireplace, and the images of the fish are
beginning to dissolve into liquid. It is now half-liquid and half-fish.
XI. The crystal coffin is completely full of liquid, and the fire is reduced to ashes.
XII. The crystal coffin is then put into the fireplace and covered with the ashes.
XIII. I see two beings. They are both androgynous; they put a crown upon the
fisherman.
XIV. The two beings put a purple and golden cloak upon the shoulders of the
fisherman.
XV. One androgynous being puts a sceptre into the right hand of the fisherman.
The other being puts an orb into the left hand of the fisherman.

135

THE FEMININE

XVI. I see the fisherman King striking the orb. The ashes which covered the coffin are beginning to divide into two.

XVII. The orb is divided into two, and out comes a great bird. Within the fire, the crystal casket has been rent asunder, and there stands a golden androgynous being.

XVIII. The fisherman King disrobes himself of his worldly finery.

XIX. He embraces the golden androgynous being. The great bird hovers above his head. He sheds his feathers, which fall upon the Fisherman King and the great androgynous being.

XX. I see the image of one small perfect diamond. Within it are the man and the woman as the Royal King and Queen. Above their heads flies a golden bird.

An Alchemical Treatise of Roger Bacon
Concerning the Regeneration of the Stone

And when you make the inner as the outer, and the outer as the inner, and the upper as the lower, and when you make male and female into a single one, so that the male shall not be male and the female shall not be female, then shall you enter the Kingdom.

Gospel of Thomas

All figures of all souls
about to be born
stand before God in pairs—
each soul and each spirit
consisting of both male and female.

They are given
to the emissary
called NIGHT,
who is in charge of conception,
and the male and female parts of the soul
unite and become one being.

After this,
they slowly descend to this earth—
though not always at the same time—
and they separate
and animate two different bodies.

At the time of marriage
the Holy One, blessed be he,
who knows all souls and all spirits,
unites them again as they were before,
and they again constitute one body and one soul,
forming as it were the right and left of one individual.
Such persons are called whole.

"The Birth of the Soul," Jerry Winston

136

In love
I feel both pain and pleasure
Which is quite clearly seen
In the nature of Dakinis.
Sometimes it is tedious,
Tedious because you're hopeful,
Hopeful for something to happen.
Sometimes it is creative
And your heart is open
To creativity.
These two manifestations
Are clearly seen
Alternatively,
Pain and pleasure alike.
It is what is.
That is what I have found.
In pain there's no sickness
Because pain is aroused
By creative forces.
Thanks to Dakinis.
The same goes for pleasure,
The same goes for love.
Love is something profound
Something deeper—
In fact it's the flow
Of the universe.
Without love nothing is created.

Chögyam Trungpa

Zero: The Mathematics of the Unborn

THE MATHEMATICAL SYMBOL or translation for the primary unborn nature of the feminine is 0 (zero). As an ordinal numeral indicating an initial point or origin, zero is related to the primordial space-womb nature of the feminine. It is the point in which unborn time and space collapse completely and is the generative midpoint between the infinite series of positive and negative numerals that extend from it; it is the primary center, the origin or fountain of mathematical possibility. Number and the different numerical relationships represent all of the different possibilities that comprise the structure of the phenomenal world. The development of the concept of zero as the fulcrum of these possibilities is a metaphysical insight of monumental proportions.

There are two world traditions in which zero has been developed as a metaphysical/mathematical concept and a symbol notation: the Babylonian Indo-Arabic-European in the Eastern hemisphere and the Olmec-Mayan in the Western. Our word *zero* seems to be derived from the Sanskrit term *sunya*, which was later transformed into the Arabic *sifr*, the Latin *zephyrum*, and then into the English words *zero* and *cipher*. The Babylonian root word is not known, although it is generally conceded that the concept and notation for zero were originally developed in Babylonia—heir to the ancient "mother" culture of Sumeria, 3000–1500 B.C.— around the third century B.C. The mathematical genius of the Sumer-Babylonians diffused to India, where it became incorporated into the grand cosmological structures of Mahayana Buddhism and the nascent forms of modern Hinduism sometime between the third century B.C. and the ninth century A.D. The earliest documented Hindu calculations utilizing zero date from the ninth century A.D. About the same time, in 825, Al-Khwarizmi of Bagdad wrote the first book on algebra which was translated into Latin around 1120 by Adelard of Bath, thus introducing the zero into European civilization.

Little is known about the shadowy Babylonian origins of the zero as concept and notation. In Buddhist-Hindu thought, the notational sign for zero is either a 0 or a •. The circular form is the one that has come down to us; in both cases, however, the symbolism is directly related to the primary feminine quality of the womb or generative space. The zero as a point—Sanskrit, *bindu*—signifies the origin or seed of the phenomenal world. As an empty circle, without beginning or end, the notation for zero symbolizes infinity. European precedent for this concept is found in the Platonic/Pythagorean notion of the circle/sphere as the perfect, ultimate form from which all other forms are generated. The Sanskrit word describing the circular notation is *sunya*, traditionally meaning vacant, void, or empty in the sense of not containing anything. This corresponds to the modern meaning of cipher and zero. Cipher carries the additional meaning of a place where something can occur. But there is also in the word *sunya* the sense of swollen, as in the idea of the womb or the swelling of generative potentiality. *Sunya,* expanded into *sunyata,* meaning the quality of *sunya* or emptiness, became one of the central concepts of Mahayana Buddhist philosophy and practice. In Buddhism *sunyata* describes the basic existential quality of things freed from all of our conceptualizations about them. It is the open dimension of being.

As openness, *sunyata* describes the inherent condition of the mind, without preconceptions, expectations, and habitual thoughts. The realization of *sunyata* gives birth to *prajna,* an intelligence that cuts through and transcends all forms of conceptualization and fixation; it is the capacity for seeing things as they are. Both *sunyata* and *prajna* are considered expressions of the feminine principle. It is through the experience of the unbounded space provided by the feminine principle that we are able to perceive the open dimension of things—and this perception is itself an exercise of *prajna,* our intuitive intelligence. *Prajnaparamita,* often translated as the Mother of all Buddhas, refers to transcendental wisdom or understanding based in the teaching of *sunyata.* The well-known Mahayana texts, the *Prajnaparamita Sutras,* contain the essential teaching of *sunyata*—zero—in one succinct verse:

> *form is emptiness*
> *emptiness itself is form*

Sunyata may also be viewed from a three-fold perspective. Seeing the world as form, seeing the world as emptiness, and seeing the inseparability of form and emptiness.

From the Mahayanist point of view, the activity that develops through the medium of intuitive wisdom, rooted in the open dimension, *sunyata,* is compassion. The Sanskrit term signifying compassion is *karuna,* which is traditionally viewed in Buddhism as a masculine quality. In the Buddhist conception it is the union of feminine space and the unceasing masculine activity of compassion flowing from that space that creates the enlightened attitude—*bodhicitta.*

> *The indivisibility of sunyata and karuna is termed bodhicitta.*
>
> sGam.po.pa

Much less is known of the metaphysical and psychological refinements of Mayan and pre-Mayan thought than is known of the early developments of philosophy and mathematics in India. From extant Mayan hieroglyphs,* however, certain parallels may be drawn between the Mayan and Indian permutations of the zero. It seems possible that the notion and notation of the zero developed even earlier in ancient Mexico than in the Indo-Sumerian region. The earliest heiroglyphic records bearing a zero notation date to the third century A.D. However, since this example already represents a fully developed tradition, a somewhat earlier date is assumed for the actual origin of zero. Since the Mayan mathematical system seems to have been derived from the more mysterious mother culture of the Olmecs (1500–300 B.C.), the ultimate derivation of the zero may extend back several centuries earlier in the new world than the Babylonian formulation in the third century B.C.

The basic Mayan conception of zero corresponds to our ideas of fullness or completeness. The term describing zero has its root in the word *lub,* which has been defined by the historian Miguel León-Portilla as: "end of the journey, place where the burden rests. It bears symbolic forms such as a shell or a hand as an attached element. Its personification is a face with traits peculiar to the god of death." *Lub* relates to several other words that help to illuminate the significance of zero in Mayan thought.

---

*A notation is a complete abstraction intended to represent numbers, qualities, or certain conceptual values. Hieroglyphics is a system of writing in which figures or objects are used to represent words or sounds.

Lubul means to fall, *lubzah* means to upset something, *lubay* means great resting place or the destination at the end of a journey. In the Kekchi dialect of the Mayan language, *lub* means tired or weary. Whereas zero in traditions of the Eastern hemisphere may mean either a total depletion or signify a space or emptiness in the sense of a generative potentiality, in the Mayan tradition zero tends to express emptiness in the sense of completion, that there is nothing more to be done, or that a situation is worn out, or ended. In terms of the primal symbolism of the feminine, we are dealing here with zero as the emblem of the great and boundless mystery of birth *and* death. A comparison of the Mayan word *lubay* with the Sanskrit word *nirvana* articulates further nuances of the feminine principle. *Nirvana* literally means blown out. But like the word *lubay* it also implies a great resting place and the destination at the end of a journey, in this case, the pursuit of wisdom. *Nirvana* as the full experience of enlightenment completes the journey begun in the ejection from the womb; insofar as *nirvana* is a blowing out, like *lubay*, it also suggests a return, a completion of the circle taking one back to primary space where there is neither beginning nor end. As embodiment of that primary space, *nirvana* is full awareness, enlightenment. Though there are numerous variants, the two basic components of the Mayan hieroglyph for zero are constant: the death head with a hand for the lower jaw. The death head expresses the idea of emptiness and expiration in the sense of a completion of a journey. The hand as shaper, container, or fulfiller symbolizes the idea of completeness or totality. The combination of the hand with the death's head is a powerful evocation of the contrasting meanings given to zero.

99.

Two mathematical notational marks for zero are found in the Mayan system: the symbol of the moon and that of the shell. The richness of the feelings and observations inspired by the moon's relentless waxing and waning, its periods of disappearance, and its points of total fullness, imply the whole range of metaphysical, mathematical, and mythological structures symbolized by zero. The more common computational notation for zero, the shell, is equally suggestive. One of the common variants is the bivalved conch, which introduces the motif of the spiral. The shell notation relates to the Indo-Arabic-European concept of the zero as a point of origin. The symbolism of the shell with its spiral motion signifying generation, corresponds with the basic feminine attribute of womb-space providing or accommodating the potential for infinite gestations. The general term for shell in Mayan is *xixim*, derived from a root *xim* or more likely *xix* which signifies *completely*. Two Mayan phrases are useful in conveying this concept: *xix ich tahte*—to look at someone from head to foot; and *xix uouol oc*—perfectly round or spherical.

100.

The different meanings given to zero in Mayan and Mahayana systems of thought point to the paradoxical coexistence of fullness and emptiness, beginning and end. Both Mahayana and Mayan thought are based on an inherently cyclical view of the universe; the zero of origins and the zero of completion are the same, for beginning and end coincide. It is through understanding the sameness of beginning and end, or whatever we think of as "opposites," that cycles of birth and death are overcome.

Since the Middle Ages in the European West, zero has been pivotal in the development of many new forms of mathematics, including calculus, Riemannian geometry, and topology. The perennial metaphysical implications of zero have continued to inform its more purely mathematical developments. In the esoteric European tradition, the Ouroboric dragon biting its own tail, symbolizing cyclical completeness and transcendence, also forms a zero. The literal meaning of universe is *one turn*, one complete cycle of a process that may be without beginning or end.

101.

Like the Ouroboros, each full turn or cycle of the universe is a totality in itself. This corresponds to the contemporary notion of the Big Bang theory of the universe, which hypothesizes that the universe is a continuous series of cycles, each beginning with a monumental explosion, expanding outward for forty billion years, and then collapsing for another forty billion. The Big Bang viewpoint comes very close to expressing the classic Hindu-Buddhist and Mayan perceptions and calculations about the nature of the cycles of the universe.

If the beginning and end of a cosmic cycle is defined as zero, the midpoint of maximum universe diffusion as the absolute equalization of expanding and contracting movements is also defined by zero. According to this point of view, the universe is isotropic: identical in all directions, therefore describing a perfect sphere whose expansions and contractions are symmetrical.

The modern astrophysical definition of the universe in terms of a zero beginning, midpoint, and end is surprisingly archaic or literally timeless. In defining the cosmological process, the modern notions of zero echo the archaic vision of the womb, the beginningless unborn condition. In the protohistoric cult of the Great Mother (10,000–3,000 B.C.), the fundamental life process was also defined as a cyclical or circular trajectory leading from zero—the womb of the Great Mother—to a point of maximum departure and then, at death, zero again, a return to the womb. The totality of the process was defined and contained by the feminine principle as symbolized by the womb, begetter of all forms and inspiration, and receptable of expiration. Because of their mutual philosophical belief in zero as the transcendence of time, it is not surprising that modern astrophysics and the ancient cult of the Great Mother describe a similar view of the universe.

Bibliography

HISTORY

Adams, Henry. *Mont-Saint-Michel.* New York: Mentor Books, 1961.

Argüelles, José. *The Transformative Vision.* Berkeley and London: Shambhala Publications, 1975.

Aston, W. G., trans. *Nihongi: Chronicles of Japan.* Vermont and Japan: Charles E. Tuttle Co., 1972.

Bachofen, J. J. *Myth, Religion and Mother Right.* Translated by Ralph Manheim. Bollingen Series, no. 84. Princeton: Princeton University Press, 1967.

Basham, A. L. *The Wonder That Was India.* New York: Macmillan Co., 1954.

Bernal, Ignacio. *The Olmec World.* Translated by Doris Heyden and Fernando Horcasitas. Berkeley: University of California Press, 1969.

Bu-ston. *History of Buddhism.* Translated by Dr. E. Obermiller. Heidelberg, 1931.

Coe, Michael D. *America's First Civilization.* New York: American Heritage Publishing Co., 1968.

Covarrubias, Miguel. *Island of Bali.* New York: Alfred A. Knopf, 1942.

Davis, Elizabeth Gould. *The First Sex.* Baltimore, Md.: Penguin Books, 1972.

Diner, Helen. *Mothers and Amazons.* New York: Doubleday & Co., 1973.

Ehrenreich, Barbara, and English, Deirdre. *Witches, Midwives and Nurses: A History of Women Healers.* New York: Feminist Press, 1973.

Eliade, Mircea. *Cosmos and History.* Translated by Willard R. Trask. New York: Harper & Row, 1959.

Evans, Sir Arthur. *The Palace of Minos at Knossos.* London and New York: Macmillan Co., 1921.

Gimbutas, Marija. *The Gods and Goddesses of Old Europe.* Berkeley and Los Angeles: University of California Press, 1974.

Hawkes, Jacquetta. *The Dawn of the Gods.* London: Chatto & Windus, 1968.

James, E. O. *The Cult of the Mother Goddess.* New York: Praeger Publishers, 1959.

Lebreton, Jules, S. J., and Zeiller, Jacques. *The Triumph of Christianity.* Book IV. Translated by E. C. Messenger. New York: Collier Books, 1962.

Levy, C. Rachel. *Religious Conceptions of the Stone Age.* New York: Harper & Row, 1963.

Marshak, Alexander. *Roots of Civilization.* New York: McGraw-Hill, 1972.

Murray, M. A. *The Witch Cult in Western Europe.* London: Oxford University Press, 1921.

Mylonas, George E. *Mycenae and the Mycenaean Age.* Princeton: Princeton University Press, 1966.

Piggott, Stuart, ed. *The Dawn of Civilization.* New York: McGraw-Hill, 1961.

Sana, Kshanika. *Buddhism and Buddhist Literature in Central Asia.* Calcutta: Mukhopadhyay, 1970.

Schliemann, Heinrich. *Mycenae.* New York: B. Blom, 1967.

Showerman, Grant. *The Great Mother of the Gods.* Philology and Literature Series, vol. 1, no. 3. *Bulletin of the University of Wisconsin,* no. 43 (1901).

Sircar, D. C., ed. *The Sakti Cult and Tārā.* Calcutta: University of Calcutta Press, 1967.

Stein, R. A. *Tibetan Civilization.* Translated by J. E. Stapleton Driver. London: Faber & Faber; Stanford, Calif.: Stanford University Press, 1972.

Stewart, Desmond, and the editors of Time-Life Books. *Early Islam.* New York: Time-Life Books, 1967.

Tompkins, Peter. *Secrets of the Great Pyramid.* New York: Harper & Row, 1971.

Weltfish, Gene. *The Lost Universe: The Way of Life of the Pawnee.* New York: Basic Books, 1965.

Zeller, Eduard. *Outlines of the History of Greek Philosophy.* New York: Meridian Books, 1955.

LITERATURE AND ART

d'Alviella, Goblet. *The Migration of Symbols.* London: Archibald Constable & Co., 1894.

Andrews, Edward D. *The Gift to Be Simple.* New York: Dover Publications, n.d.

Anton, Ferdinand. *Women in Pre-Columbian America.* New York: Abner Schram, 1955.

Argüelles, José. *Charles Henry and the Formation of a Psychophysical Aesthetic.* Chicago and London: University of Chicago Press, 1972.

Argüelles, José and Argüelles, Miriam T. *Mandala.* Berkeley and London: Shambhala Publications, 1972.

Astrov, Margot, ed. *American Indian Prose and Poetry.* New York: Capricorn Books, 1962.

de Beauvoir, Simone. *The Second Sex.* Translated by H. M. Parshley. New York: Alfred A. Knopf, 1957.

Beurdeley, Michael; Schipper, Krisotofer; Fu-Jui, Chang; and Pimpaneau, Jacques. *Chinese Erotic Art.* Rutland, Vt. and Tokyo: Charles E. Tuttle Co., 1969.

Blake, William. *Blake: Complete Writing*. Edited by Geoffrey Keynes. New York and London: Oxford University Press, 1966.

Boer, Charles. *The Homeric Hymns*. Chicago: Swallow Press, 1970.

Breton, André. *Manifestos of Surrealism*. Ann Arbor: University of Michigan Press, 1969.

Burckhardt, Titus. *Art of Islam: Language and Meaning*. London: World of Islam Publishing Co., 1976.

Burnham, Jack. *Great Western Salt Works: Essays on the Meaning of Post-Formalist Art*. New York: George Braziller, 1974.

Chang, Garma C. C., trans. *The Hundred Thousand Songs of Milarepa*. 2 vols. New York: University Books, 1962.

Chung-yuan, Chang. *Creativity and Taoism*. New York: Julian Press, 1963.

Cirlot, J. E. *A Dictionary of Symbols*. Translated by Jack Sage. New York: Philosophical Library, 1962.

Coomaraswamy, Ananda K. *Elements of Buddhist Iconography*. New Delhi: Munishram Manoharlal, 1972.

Crawford, I. M. *The Art of the Wandjina*. London: Oxford University Press, 1968.

Dante Alighieri. *The Divine Comedy*. Translated by Carlyle-Wicksteed. New York: Vintage Books, 1950.

Devendra, D. T. *Guide of Anuradhapura*. Colombo, 1952.

Dickinson, Emily. *The Poems of Emily Dickinson*. Edited by Martha Dickinson Bianchi and Alfred Leete Hampson. Boston: Little, Brown & Co., 1934.

Doolittle, Hilda [H. D.]. *Selected Poems*. New York: Grove Press, 1957.

E. B. Crocker Art Gallery. *The Huichol Creation of the World*. Sacramento: E. B. Crocker Art Gallery, 1975.

Fernandez, Justino. *Coatlicue*. 2 vols. Baltimore, Md.: Penguin Books, 1955.

Fulcanelli. *Le Mystère des Cathédrales*. Translated by Mary Sworder. London: Neville Spearman, 1971.

Gauguin, Paul. *Noa Noa*. New York: Noonday Press, 1957.

Giedion, Sigfried. *The Eternal Present*. Vol. I, *The Beginnings of Art*. Vol. II, *The Beginnings of Architecture*. Bollingen Series, no. 35. Princeton: Princeton University Press, 1964.

Goethe, Johann Wolfgang von. *Faust*. Translated by Louis MacNeice. London: Oxford University Press, 1951.

Govinda, Lama Anagarika. *Psychocosmic Symbolism of the Buddhist Stupa*. Emeryville, Calif.: Dharma Publishing, 1976.

Grunwedel, Albert. *Buddhist Art in India*. London: Bhartiya Publishing House, 1974.

Haggard, H. Rider. *Three Adventure Novels*. New York: Dover Publications, 1951.

Hardenberg, Friedrich Philipp von [Novalis]. *Hymns to the Night*. Translated by Charles E. Passage. Indianapolis and New York: Bobbs-Merrill Co., 1960.

Heilbrun, Carolyn G. *Toward a Recognition of Androgyny*. New York: Alfred A. Knopf, 1973.

Hesse, Herman. *The Journey to the East*. Translated by Hilda Rosner. New York: Noonday Press, 1957.

Homer. *The Odyssey*. Translated by E. V. Rieu. Baltimore, Md., Harmondsworth, and Sydney: Penguin Books, 1946.

James, Edwin Oliver. *From Cave to Cathedral: Temples and Shrines of Prehistoric Classical and Early Christian Times*. New York: Praeger Publishers, 1965.

Karunaratne, T. B. *The Buddhist Wheel Symbol*. Kandy, Ceylon: Buddhist Publication Society, 1969.

Katzenellenbogen, Adolf. *The Sculptural Programs of Chartres Cathedral*. Baltimore, Md.: Johns Hopkins University Press, 1959.

Keeler, Clyde E. *Cuna Indian Art*. New York: Exposition Press, 1969.

Klee, Paul. *Diaries 1898–1918*. Berkeley and Los Angeles: University of California Press, 1964.

Kupka, Karel. *Dawn of Art: Paintings and Sculpture of Australian Aborigines*. New South Wales: Angus & Robertson, 1965.

Lawrence, David Herbert. *The Collected Poems of D. H. Lawrence*. Introduction by Kenneth Rexroth. New York: New Directions, 1948.

————. *Sons and Lovers*. New York: Harper, 1951.

LeGuin, Ursula K. *The Left Hand of Darkness*. New York: Ace Books, 1976.

León-Portilla, Miguel. *Pre-Columbian Literatures of Mexico*. Norman, Okla.: University of Oklahoma Press, 1969.

Lessing, Doris. *Briefing for a Descent into Hell*. New York: Alfred A. Knopf, 1971.

————. *The Golden Notebook*. New York: Simon & Schuster, 1962.

Lommel, Andreas. *Prehistoric and Primitive Man*. New York: McGraw-Hill, 1966.

————. *Shamanism: The Beginnings of Art*. New York and Toronto: McGraw-Hill, 1967.

Maitreya 4: Woman. Berkeley and London: Shambhala Publications, 1973.

Matthews, W. H. *Mazes and Labyrinths*. London: Longmans, Greene & Co., 1922.

McCarthy, Mary. *Memories of a Catholic Girlhood*. New York: Harcourt Brace, 1957.

Mookerjee, Ajit. *Tantra Art: Its Philosophy and Physics*. New York, New Delhi, and Paris: Ravi Kumar, 1966.

————. *Tantra Asana*. Basel, Paris, and New Delhi: Ravi Kumar, 1971.

THE FEMININE

Moore, Marianne. *Collected Poems.* New York: Macmillan Co., 1967.

Mountford, Charles P. *Art, Myth and Symbolism.* Records of the American-Australian Scientific Expedition to Arnheim Land, vol. I. Melbourne: Melbourne University Press, 1956.

Murray, Michele. *The Great Mother and Other Poems.* New York: Sheed Andrews & McMeel, 1974.

Nin, Anaïs. *The Diary of Anaïs Nin.* Edited by Gunther Stuhlmann. New York: Swallow Press and Harcourt Brace Jovanovich, 1966.

Panofsky, Erwin. *Meaning in the Visual Arts.* New York: Doubleday & Co., 1957.

Piankoff, Alexandre, trans. *The Shrine of Tut-Anhk-Amon.* The Bollingen Library. New York: Pantheon Books, 1955.

de Prima, Diane. *Loba.* Part I. Santa Barbara, Calif.: Capra Press, 1973.

Prinz, Hugo. *Altorientalische Symbolik.* Berlin: Karl Curtius, 1915.

Purce, Jill. *The Mystic Spiral.* New York: Avon Books; London: Thames & Hudson, 1974.

Rawson, Philip, and Legeza, Laszlo. *Tao.* New York: Avon Books; London: Thames & Hudson, 1973.

Rice, David Talbot. *Islamic Art.* New York: Praeger Publishers, 1965.

Rowland, Benjamin. *The Art and Architecture of India.* Baltimore, Md.: Penguin Books, 1967.

Schwaller de Lubicz, Isha. *Her-Bak.* Translated by Lucie Lamy. 2 vols. London: Hodder & Stoughton, 1954.

Scully, Vincent. *The Earth, the Temple and the Gods: Greek Sacred Architecture.* New York and London: Praeger Publishers, 1969.

Shah, Idries. *The Sufis.* Translated by Robert Graves. New York: Doubleday & Co., 1964.

Spink, Walter. *The Axis of Eros.* New York: Shocken Books, 1973.

Stones, Bones, and Skin: Ritual and Shamanic Art. Arts Canada, December 1973–January 1974.

Suzuki, D. T. *Zen and Japanese Culture.* Bollingen Series, vol. 64. Princeton: Princeton University Press, 1970.

Sweeny, James Johnson. *Joan Miró.* New York: Museum of Modern Art, 1941.

Trungpa, Chögyam. *Mudra.* Berkeley and London: Shambhala Publications, 1972.

_____. *Visual Dharma: The Buddhist Art of Tibet.* Berkeley and London: Shambhala Publications, 1975.

Wilson, Thomas. "The Swastika." *Smithsonian Institution Annual Report.* Washington, D. C.: Smithsonian Institution Press, 1893–94.

_____. "Prehistoric Art." *Smithsonian Institution Annual Report.* Washington, D. C.: Smithsonian Institution Press, 1895–96.

Winston, Jerry. *Colors from the Zohar.* San Francisco: Barah, 1976.

Wosien, Maria Gabrielle. *Sacred Dance.* New York: Avon Books; London: Thames & Hudson, 1974.

Yeats, William Butler. *A Vision.* London: Macmillan & Co., 1962; New York: Macmillan Co., 1966.

MYTHS AND RELATED STUDIES

Alexander, Hartley Burr. *The World's Rim.* Lincoln, Neb.: University of Nebraska Press, 1967.

Andersen, Hans Christian. *The Complete Fairytales and Stories.* Translated by E. C. Havgaard. New York: Doubleday & Co., 1974.

Budge, E. A. Wallis. *The Gods of the Egyptians.* 2 vols. Chicago: Open Court Publishing Co.; London: Metheun & Co., 1904.

Campbell, Joseph. *The Hero with a Thousand Faces.* Bollingen Series, no. 17. Princeton: Princeton University Press, 1968.

_____. *The Masks of God.* 4 vols. New York: Viking Press, 1959–1968.

_____, ed. *The Mysteries. Papers from the Eranos Yearbooks,* vol. 2. Bollingen Series, no. 30, Princeton: Princeton University Press, 1955.

_____. *The Mythic Image.* Bollingen Series, no. 100. Princeton: Princeton University Press, 1975.

_____. *Myths to Live By.* New York: Viking Press, 1972.

_____, ed. *Pagan and Christian Mysteries.* Translated by Ralph Manheim and R. F. C. Hull. New York: Harper & Row and Bollingen Library, 1955.

Coomaraswamy, Ananda, and Sister Nivedita. *Myths of the Hindus and Buddhists.* London: Constable & Co.; New York: Dover Publications, 1967.

Courlander, Harold. *Tales of Yoruba Gods and Heroes.* New York: Crown Publishers, 1973.

Crawford, O. G. S. *The Eye Goddess.* London: Phoenix House, 1957.

Eliade, Mircea. *Gods, Goddesses, and Myths of Creation.* New York: Harper & Row, 1974.

_____. *Myths, Dreams, and Mysteries.* London: Harvill Press; New York: Harper & Row, 1960.

_____. *The Two and the One.* Translated by J. M. Cohen. London: Harvill Press; New York: Harper & Row, 1965.

von Franz, Marie-Louise. *An Introduction to the Interpretation of Fairytales.* New York and Zurich: Spring Publications, 1970.

_____. *Problems of the Feminine in Fairytales.* New York and Zurich: Spring Publications, 1972.

Fraser, J. G. *The Golden Bough.* London: Macmillan & Co., 1922.

Grant, Michael. *Myths of Greeks and Romans.* London: Weidenfeld & Nicolson, 1962.

Graves, Robert. *The White Goddess.* New York: Farrar, Straus & Giroux, 1973.

Grimm, Jakob Ludwig Karl. *Grimm's Fairy Tales.* New York: Pantheon Books, 1944.

Haile, Father Berard, O. F. M. *Emergence Myth, According to the Hanelthnaghe or Upward-Reaching Rite.* Santa Fe, N. M.: Museum of Navajo Ceremonial Art, 1949.

Hamilton, Edith. *Mythology.* Boston: Little, Brown & Co., 1942.

James, T. G. H. *Myths and Legends of Ancient Egypt.* London: Hamlyn Publishing, 1969.

Jung, C. G., and Kerenyi, C. *Essays on a Science of Mythology.* Translated by R. F. C. Hull. New York: Harper & Row, 1963.

Keeler, Clyde E. *Apples of Immortality from the Cuna Tree of Life.* New York: Exposition Press, 1961.

_____. *Secrets of the Cuna Earthmother.* New York: Exposition Press, 1960.

MacKenzie, Donald A. *The Migration of Symbols and their Relations to Beliefs and Customs.* London: Kegan Paul Trench, Trubner; New York: Alfred Knopf, 1926.

_____. *Myths and Traditions of the South Sea Islands.* London: Gresham Publishing Co., 1914.

_____. *Myths of Crete and Pre-Hellenic Europe.* London: Gresham Publishing Co., 1917.

Malinowski, Bronislav. *Sex, Culture and Myth.* London: Hart-Davis, 1963.

Mead, Margaret. *From the South Seas: Studies of Adolescence and Sex in Primitive Societies.* New York: William Morrow & Co., 1930.

Mylonas, G. *Eleusis and the Eleusinian Mysteries.* Princeton: Princeton University Press, 1961.

Nicholson, Irene. *Mexican and Central American Mythology.* London: Hamlyn Publishing, 1967.

Niethammer, Carolyn. *Daughters of the Earth: Lives and Legends of American Indian Women.* New York: Macmillan Co.; London: Macmillan & Co., 1977.

Parrinder, Geoffrey. *African Mythology.* London: Hamlyn Publishing, 1967.

Poignant, Roslyn. *Oceanic Mythology.* London: Hamlyn Publishing, 1967.

Radin, Paul. *The Trickster: A Study in American Indian Mythology.* London: Routledge & Kegan Paul, 1956.

Reiser, Oliver L. *This Holyest Erthe: The Glastonbury Zodiac and King Arthur's Camelot.* London: Perennial Books, 1974.

Sandars, N. K., trans. *The Epic of Gilgamesh.* Baltimore, Md. and Middlesex: Penguin Books, 1960.

Schafer, Edward H. *The Divine Woman.* Berkeley, Los Angeles, and London: University of California Press, 1973.

Slater, Philip E. *The Glory of Hera.* Boston: Beacon Press, 1968.

Zimmer, Heinrich. *The King and the Corpse.* Edited by Joseph Campbell. Cleveland and New York: Meridian Books, 1960.

_____. *Myths and Symbols in Indian Art.* Edited by Joseph Campbell. Bollingen Series, vol. 6. Princeton: Princeton University Press, 1971.

Zuntz, Günther. *Persephone.* Oxford at Clarendon: Oxford University Press, 1971.

PHILOSOPHY AND RELIGION

Asvaghosa. *The Awakening of Faith.* Translated by Y. S. Hakeda. New York and London: Columbia University Press, 1967.

Beyer, Stephan. *The Cult of Tara.* Berkeley and Los Angeles: The University of California Press, 1973.

Bingen, Hildegard von. *Wisse Die Wege: Scivias.* Salzburg; Otto Müllerverlag, 1954.

Black Elk. *The Sacred Pipe.* Edited by Joseph E. Brown. Norman, Okla.: University of Oklahoma Press, 1953.

Blakney, Raymond Bernard. *Meister Eckhart.* New York: Harper & Row, 1941.

Blavatsky, M. P. *The Secret Doctrine.* Wheaton, Ill., Madras, India, and London: Theosophical Publishing House, 1888.

Blofeld, John. *The Zen Teaching of Huang Po.* New York: Grove Press, 1958.

Buddhaghosa, Bhadantacariya. *The Path of Purification (Visuddhimagga).* Translated by Bhikku Nyanamoli. Colombo: A. Semage, 1964.

Budge, E. A. Wallis. *The Book of the Dead.* New York: Barnes & Noble, n. d.

_____. *The Egyptian Heaven and Hell.* LaSalle, Ill.: Open Court Publishing Co., 1925.

Burckhardt, Titus. *Alchemy, Science of the Cosmos, Science of the Soul.* Translated by William Stoddart. London: Stuart & Watkins, 1967; Baltimore, Md.: Penguin Books, 1972.

_____. *An Introduction to Sufi Doctrine.* Translated by D. M. Matheson. Lahore: Sh. Muhammad Ashraf, 1959.

Busteed, Marilyn, et al. *Phases of the Moon.* Berkeley and London: Shambhala Publications, 1974.

THE FEMININE   Chang, Garma C. C. *The Buddhist Teaching of Totality*. University Park, Pa. and London: Pennsylvania State University Press, 1971.

Chaudhuri, Haridas, and Spiegelberg, Frederic, eds. *The Integral Philosophy of Sri Aurobindo*. London: George Allen & Unwin, 1960.

Conze, Edward, trans. and ed. *Buddhist Wisdom Books*. London: George Allen & Unwin, 1958; New York and London: Harper & Row, 1972.

————, trans. and ed. *The Perfection of Wisdom in Eight Thousand Lines and Its Verse Summary*. Bolinas, Calif.: Four Seasons Foundation, 1973.

Corbin, Henry. *Creative Imagination in the Sufism of Ibn' Arabi*. Translated by R. Manheim. Bollingen Series, vol. 91. Princeton: Princeton University Press, 1969.

Cumont, Franz. *Astrology and Religion Among the Greeks and Romans*. London: Constable & Co.; New York: Dover Publications, 1960.

Daniélou, Alan. *Hindu Polytheism*. Bollingen Series, vol. 73. Princeton: Princeton University Press, 1964.

Dasgupta, Shasti Bhusan. *An Introduction to Tantric Buddhism*. Berkeley and London: Shambhala Publications, 1974.

De Rola, Stanislas Klossowski. *Alchemy*. New York: Avon Books; London: Thames & Hudson, 1973.

Eliade, Mircea. *The Forge and the Crucible*. Translated by Stephen Corrin. London: Rider & Co. 1962; New York: Harper & Row, 1971.

————. *Patterns in Comparative Religion*. London: Sheed & Ward, 1958; Cleveland and New York: World Publishing Co., 1963.

————. *Rites and Symbols of Initiation*. New York: Harper & Row, 1965.

————. *Shamanism*. Translated by Willard R. Trask. Bollingen Series, vol. 76. Princeton: Princeton University Press, 1964.

————. *Yoga: Immortality and Freedom*. Translated by Willard R. Trask. Bollingen Series, vol. 56. New York: Pantheon Books, 1958.

Evans-Wentz, W. Y. *The Tibetan Book of the Great Liberation*. London: Oxford University Press, 1954.

Forrester-Brown, James S. *The Two Creation Stories in Genesis*. Berkeley and London: Shambhala Publications, 1974.

Frankfort, H; Frankfort, H. A.; Wilson, John A.; Jacobsen, Thorkild. *Before Philosophy*. Chicago: University of Chicago Press, 1946.

Fremantle, Francesca, and Trungpa, Chögyam, trans. *The Tibetan Book of the Dead*. Berkeley and London: Shambhala Publications, 1975.

Gam.Po.Pa. *The Jewel Ornament of Liberation*. Translated by Herbert V. Guenther. Berkeley and London: Shambhala Publications, 1971.

Ghose, Aurobindo. *Sri Aurobindo on Himself and the Mother*. Pondicherry: Sri Aurobindo Ashram, 1953.

Goddard, Dwight, ed. *A Buddhist Bible*. New York: E. P. Dutton & Co., 1966.

Griaule, Marcel. *Conversations with Ogotemmêli*. London: Oxford University Press, 1975.

Guenther, Herbert V. *The Life and Teachings of Naropa*. London and New York: Oxford University Press, 1963.

————. *The Tantric View of Life*. Berkeley and London: Shambhala Publications, 1972.

————. *Treasures on the Tibetan Middle Way*. Berkeley and London: Shambhala Publications, 1969.

Guenther, Herbert V., and Kawamura, Leslie S. *Mind in Buddhist Psychology*. Emeryville, Calif.: Dharma Publishing, 1975.

Guenther, Herbert V., and Trungpa, Chögyam. *The Dawn of Tantra*. Berkeley and London: Shambhala Publications, 1975.

Hall, Manly P. *The Secret Teachings of All Ages*. Los Angeles: Philosophical Research Society, 1969.

Harrison, Jane. *Prolegomena to the Study of Greek Religion*. London: Cambridge University Press, 1903.

Hesiod. *Theogony*. Translated by Norman O. Brown. New York: Liberal Arts Press, 1953.

Holy Bible. King James Version. Newton Upper Falls, Mass.: Pathmark Books, 1973.

Humphreys, Christmas. *Concentration and Meditation*. London: John M. Watkins, 1959.

Huxley, Aldous. *The Perennial Philosophy*. Cleveland and New York: McGraw-Hill, 1972.

I Ching. Translated by Richard Wilhelm and Cary F. Baynes. Bollingen Series, no. 19. Princeton: Princeton University Press, 1967.

Jerusalem Bible. Edited by Alexander Jones. New York: Doubleday & Co., 1967.

Kelsey, M. T. *The Other Side of Silence: A Guide to Christian Meditation*. Paramus, N. J.: Paulist-Newman, 1976.

Lao Tzu. *Tao Te Ching*. Translated by D. C. Lau. London and Baltimore, Md.: Penguin Books, 1963.

Lauf, Detlef. *Secret Doctrines of the Tibetan Books of the Dead*. Translated by Graham Parkes. Boulder and London: Shambhala Publications, 1977.

Legge, James, trans. *The Texts of Taoism*. 2 vols. London: Oxford University Press, 1891; New York: Dover Publications, 1962.

León-Portilla, Miguel. *Aztec Thought and Culture*. Translated by J. E. Davis. Norman, Okla.: University of Oklahoma Press, 1963.

————. *Time and Reality in the Thought of the Maya*. Translated by Charles L. Boiles. Boston: Beacon Press, 1973.

Maharshi, Ramana. *Collected Works*. Edited by Arthur Osborne. London and New York: Rider & Co., 1959.

Matics, Marion L. *Entering the Path of Enlightenment*. New York and London: Macmillan Co., 1970.

Merton, Thomas. *The Silent Life*. New York: Farrar, Straus & Giroux, 1975.

Mi-Pham, Lama. *Calm and Clear*. Translated by Herbert V. Guenther. Emeryville, Calif.: Dharma Publishing, 1973.

Nicholson, Reynold A. *The Mystics of Islam*. London: George Bell & Sons, 1914.

Nikhilananda, Swami. *The Upanishads*. London: George Allen & Unwin, 1963; New York: Harper & Row, 1964.

Northrup, F. S. C. *The Meeting of East and West*. New York: Macmillan Co., 1946.

Ouspensky, P. D. *A New Model of the Universe*. New York: Alfred A. Knopf, 1943.

Plato. *Timaeus*. Translated by Francis M. Cornford. New York: Liberal Arts, 1959.

————. *The Works of Plato*. Translated by Benjamin Jowett. 5 vols. London: Oxford University Press, 1892.

Poncé, Charles. *Kabbalah*. San Francisco: Straight Arrow Books, 1973.

Price, A. F., and Mou-Lam, Wong, trans. *The Diamond Sutra and the Sutra of Hui Neng*. Forewords by W. Y. Evans-Wentz, J. Miller, and C. Humphreys. Berkeley and London: Shambhala Publications, 1969.

Radin, Paul. *Primitive Religion*. New York: Dover Publications, 1957.

————. *The Road of Life and Death*. Bollingen Series, vol. 5. Princeton: Princeton University Press, 1973.

Reymond, Lizelle. *To Live Within*. New York: Doubleday & Co.; London: George Allen & Unwin, 1971.

St. Teresa. *The Life of Saint Teresa of Avila*. Translated by J. M. Cohen. Baltimore, Md. and Middlesex: Penguin Books, 1957.

Schaya, Leo. *The Universal Meaning of the Kabbalah*. Translated by Nancy Pearson. London: George Allen & Unwin, 1971; Baltimore, Md.: Penguin Books, 1973.

Scholem, Gersham G. *Major Trends in Jewish Mysticism*. New York: Schocken Books, 1961.

Séjourné, Laurette. *Burning Water*. New York: Vanguard Press, 1956; Berkeley and London: Shambhala Publications, 1976.

Seligman, Kurt. *Magic, Supernaturalism and Religion*. New York: Pantheon Books, 1948.

Shapiro, Herman, and Curley, Edwin M., eds. *Hellenistic Philosophy*. New York: Modern Library, 1965.

Slade, Herbert. *Exploration Into Contemplative Prayer*. Paramus, N. J.: Paulist-Newman, 1976.

Stcherbatsky, Theodore. *The Conception of Buddhist Nirvana*. New Delhi: Bharatiya Vidya Prakashan Publishing, 1975.

Streng, Frederick J. *Emptiness*. Nashville, Tenn.: Abingdon Press, 1967.

Suarès, Carlos. *The Cipher of Genesis*. London: Robinson & Watkins; Berkeley and London: Shambhala Publications, 1970.

————. *The Resurrection of the Word*. Berkeley and London: Shambhala Publications, 1975.

Suzuki, Shunryu. *Zen Mind, Beginner's Mind*. New York and Tokyo: Weatherhill, 1970.

Texts of the Navaho Creation Chants. Cambridge, Mass.: Peabody Museum of Harvard University, n. d.

Thera, Nyanaponika. *The Heart of Buddhist Meditation*. New York: Samuel Weiser, 1970.

Trungpa, Chögyam. *Cutting Through Spiritual Materialism*. Berkeley and London: Shambhala Publications, 1973.

————, ed. *The Foundations of Mindfulness*. Garuda IV. Berkeley and London: Shambhala Publications, 1976.

————. *Meditation in Action*. Berkeley and London: Shambhala Publications, 1970.

————. *The Myth of Freedom*. Berkeley and London: Shambhala Publications, 1976.

Underhill, Evelyn. *Mysticism*. London: Methuen & Co., 1919.

Waddell, L. Austine, *Tibetan Buddhism*. London: W. H. Allen & Co., 1895; New York: Dover Publications, 1972.

Waters, Frank, *Masked Gods*. New York: Ballantine Books, 1970.

Wheelwright, Philip. *Heraclitus*. Princeton: Princeton University Press, 1959.

Woodroffe, John [Sir Arthur Avalon]. *The Great Liberation*. Madras: Ganesh & Co., 1971.

————, trans. *Hymns to the Goddess*. Hollywood, Ca.: Vedanta Press, 1973.

Yates, Frances. *The Rosicrucian Enlightenment*. London: Routledge & Kegan Paul, 1972.

Yü, Lu K'uan. *Taoist Yoga*. New York: Samuel Weiser, 1970.

Zalman, Rabbi S. Z., of Liadi. *Likutei Amarim*. 2 vols. New York: Nissan Mindel, 1969.

PSYCHOLOGY AND STUDIES OF THE FEMININE

Borghese, Elisabeth Mann. *Ascent of Woman*. New York: George Braziller, 1963.

Briffault, Robert. *The Mothers*. London: George Allen & Unwin, 1959.

Brown, Norman O. *Life Against Death*. New York: Random House, 1959.

————. *Love's Body*. New York: Random House, 1966.

de Castillejo, Irene Claremont. *Knowing Woman*. New York: G. P. Putnam's Sons; 1973; Harper & Row, 1974.

Farber, Seymour, and Wilson, Roger L., eds. *The Potential of Woman*. New York and London: McGraw-Hill, 1963.

Flügel, J. C. *The Psycho-analytic Study of the Family*. London: Hogarth Press, 1931.

Freud, Sigmund. *Civilization and its Discontents*. Translated by Joan Riviere. London: Hogarth Press, 1957; New York: Doubleday & Co., 1958.

————. *The Interpretation of Dreams*. Translated and edited by James Strachey. London: George Allen & Unwin and Hogarth Press, 1955; New York: Science Editions, 1961.

————. *Moses and Monotheism*. Translated by Katherine Jones. London: Hogarth Press, 1951; New York: Vintage Books, 1959.

Grof, Stanislav. *Realms of the Human Unconscious*. New York: Viking Press, 1975.

Harding, M. Esther. *The Way of All Women*. New York: G. P. Putnam's Sons, 1970; London: Rider & Co., 1971.

————. *Woman's Mysteries*. New York: G. P. Putnam's Sons, 1971.

Hillman, James. *The Myth of Analysis*. Evanston, Ill.: Northwestern University Press, 1972.

Jung, Emma. *Animus and Anima*. Zurich: Spring Publications, 1972.

Jung, C. G. *Four Archetypes*. Translated by R. F. C. Hull. Bollingen Series, vol. 20. Princeton: Princeton University Press, 1971.

————. *Mysterium Coinunctionis*. Collected Works, vol. 14. Translated by R. F. C. Hull. Princeton: Princeton University Press, 1970.

————. *Psychology and Alchemy*. Collected Works, vol. 12. Translated by R. F. C. Hull. Princeton: Princeton University Press, 1968.

————. *Psychology and Religion: East and West*. Collected Works, vol. 11. Translated by R. F. C. Hull. Princeton: Princeton University Press, 1969.

————. *Symbols of Transformation*. Bollingen Series, no. 20. Princeton: Princeton University Press, 1976.

Kerenyi, C. *Eleusis: Archetypal Image of Mother and Daughter. Archetypal Images in Greek Religion*, vol. 4. Bollingen Series, vol. 65. Princeton: Princeton University Press, 1967.

Mander, Anica Vesel, and Rush, Anne Kent. *Feminism As Therapy*. Berkeley and New York: Bookworks and Random House, 1974.

Mead, Margaret. *Male and Female: A Study of the Sexes in a Changing World*. New York: William Morrow & Co., 1949.

Mellon, Joan. *Marilyn Monroe*. New York: Pyramid Publications, 1973.

Montague, Ashley. *The Natural Superiority of Women*. New York: Macmillan Co., 1954.

Neumann, Erich. *Amor and Psyche*. Translated by Ralph Manheim. New York: Pantheon Books, 1956.

————. *The Great Mother*. Translated by Ralph Manheim. Bollingen Series, vol. 47. Princeton: Princeton University Press, 1972.

————. "On the Moon and Matriarchal Consciousness." In *Fathers and Mothers*. Zurich: Spring Publications, 1973.

————. *The Origins of Consciousness*. Translated by R. F. C. Hull. Bollingen Series, vol. 42. Princeton: Princeton University Press, 1970.

Ornstein, Robert E. *The Psychology of Consciousness*. San Francisco: W. H. Freeman & Co., 1972.

Perry, John Weir. *The Self in Psychotic Process*. Berkeley and Los Angeles: University of California Press, 1953.

Rank, Otto, *The Myth of the Birth of the Hero*. Translated by F. Robins and S. E. Jelliffe. Nervous Mental Disease Monograph Series, no. 8. New York: Johnson Reprint Corp., 1941.

Reich, Wilhelm. *The Function of the Orgasm*. New York: Noonday Press, 1942.

Remen, Naomi. *The Feminine Principle, The Masculine Principle and Humanistic Medicine*. San Francisco: Institute for the Study of Humanistic Medicine, 1975.

Roszak, Betty, and Roszak, Theodore, eds. *Masculine/Feminine: Readings in Sexual Mythology and the Liberation of Woman*. New York: Harper & Row, 1970.

Singer, June. *Androgyny*. New York: Doubleday & Co., 1976.

Ulanov, Ann Belford. *The Feminine*. Evanston, Ill.: Northwestern University Press, 1971.

Watts, Alan. *Nature, Man, and Woman*. New York: Pantheon Books, 1958.

Weaver, Rix. *The Old Wise Woman*. C. G. Jung Foundation. New York: G. P. Putnam's Sons, 1973.

Whitmont, Edward Christopher. *The Symbolic Quest*. C. G. Jung Foundation for Analytical Psychology. New York: G. P. Putnam's Sons, 1969.

Woolf, Virginia. *A Room of One's Own*. New York: Harcourt, Brace & World, 1920.

SCIENCE

Berrill, N. J. *Sex and the Nature of Things*. New York: Dodd, Mead & Co., 1953.

Bohr, Niels. *Atomic Physics and Human Knowledge*. New York: Science Editions, 1961.

Bonner, John Tyler. *Morphogenesis*. Princeton: Princeton University Press, 1952.

Brown, G. Spencer. *Laws of Form*. London: George Allen & Unwin, 1969.

Calder, Nigel. *Violent Universe*. New York: Viking Press, 1969.

Capra, Fritjof. *The Tao of Physics*. Berkeley and London: Shambhala Publications, 1975.

Dampier, W. C. *A History of Science and its Relation to Philosophy and Religion*. Cambridge: At the University Press, 1966.

Goldsmith, Donald. *The Universe*. Menlo Park and London: W. A. Benjamin. 1976.

Harwit, Martin. *Astrophysical Concepts*. New York and London: John Wiley & Sons, 1973.

Heisenberg, Werner. *Physics and Philosophy*. New York: Harper & Row, 1962.

Hey, J. S. *The Radio Universe*. Oxford and New York: Pergamon Press, 1971.

Lederer, Wolfgang. *Fear of Women*. New York: Grune & Stratton, 1968.

Lovell, Sir Bernard. "In the Centre of Immensities." *Advancement of Science*. London, 29 August 1975, pp. 2–6.

Makemson, Maud Worcester. *The Morningstar Rises*. New Haven: Yale University Press; London: Oxford University Press, 1941.

Merleau-Ponty, Jacques, and Morandi, Bruno. *The Rebirth of Cosmology*. New York: Alfred A. Knopf, 1976.

Murchie, Guy. *Music of the Spheres*. 2 vols. New York: Houghton Mifflin Co., 1961.

Nasr, Seyyid Hossein. *Islamic Science*. London: World of Islam Festival Publishing Co., 1976.

Needleman, Jacob. *A Sense of the Cosmos: The Encounter of Modern Science and Ancient Truth*. New York: Doubleday & Co., 1975.

Oppenheimer, J. R. *Science and the Common Understanding*. New York: Oxford University Press, 1954.

Reiser, Oliver L. *Cosmic Humanism*. Cambridge, Mass.: Schenkman Publishing Co., 1966.

Shipman, Harry L. *Black Holes, Quasars, and the Universe*. Boston and London: Houghton Mifflin Co., 1976.

Shklovsky, I. S., and Sagan, Carl. *Intelligent Life in the Universe*. New York: Dell Publishing Co., 1966.

Verschuur, Gerit. *Starscapes: Topics in Astronomy*. Boston and Toronto: Little, Brown & Co., 1977.

Whyte, Lancelot Law, ed. *Aspects of Form*. London: Percy Lund Humphries & Co., 1951; New York: Farrar, Straus & Cudahy, 1951.

Credits

Page 108. Selection from *Letters to a Young Poet* by Rainer Maria Rilke, translated by M. D. Herter-Norton. Copyright 1954 by W. W. Norton & Company, Inc. and the Hogarth Press, Ltd. Reprinted by permission of the publishers.

Page 122. Selection from *To Live Within* by Lizelle Reymond, translated by Nancy Pearson and Stanley Speigelberg. Copyright 1971 by Doubleday & Company, Inc. Reprinted by permission of Doubleday & Company, Inc. and George Allen & Unwin, Ltd.

Pages 122 and 126. Selection from *The I Ching or Book of Changes*, translated by Richard Wilhelm, rendered into English by Cary F. Baynes. Bollingen Series XIX, third edition. Copyright 1950, 1967 by Princeton University Press. Reprinted by permission of Princeton University Press and Routledge & Kegan Paul.

Page 123. Selection from *The Sacred Pipe: Black Elk's Account of the Seven Rites of the Oglala Sioux* recorded and edited by Joseph Epes Brown. Copyright 1953 by the University of Oklahoma Press: Reprinted by permission of the publishers.

Page 125. Selection from *The Epic of Gilgamesh* translated by N. K. Sandars, 1972 edition, pp. 74-75. Copyright 1960, 1964, 1972 by N. K. Sandars. Reprinted by permission of Penguin Books, Ltd.

Pages 129-130. Selection from *The Jerusalem Bible*. Copyright 1966 by Darton, Longman & Todd, Ltd. and Doubleday & Company, Inc. Reprinted by permission of the publishers.

Pages 133-134. *Prajnaparamita Hridaya Sutra*, or *The Sutra of Transcendent Knowledge*. Reprinted by special arrangement with Vajradhatu, Boulder, Colorado.

Pages 135-136. *An Alchemical Treatise of Roger Bacon concerning the Regeneration of the Stone*. Reprinted by special arrangement with Seymour Locks.

Page 136. Selection from "The Birth of the Soul," from *Colors of the Zohar* by Jerry Winston. Reprinted by permission of Barah Publishing.

Page 137. Selection from an untitled poem in *Mudra* by Chögyam Trungpa. Reprinted by special arrangement with Chögyam Trungpa.

ILLUSTRATIONS

1. *Grey Line with Black, Blue and Yellow.* Ca. 1923. Georgia O'Keeffe. Oil on canvas. 48 X 30 inches. Courtesy of Georgia O'Keeffe. Private collection.
2. *Hole through the Sky.* Photograph by Eberhard Otto for "Stones, Bones and Skin: Ritual and Shamanic Art," *artscanada*, December 1973/January 1974.
3. Nebulosity in Monoceros. Photographed in red light. 200 inch photograph.
4. Illustration of the Aristotelian coagulum of blood and seed in the uterus, from *De Conceptu et Generatione Hominis*. Jacob Rueff, 1554.
5. Earth Goddess giving birth. Aztec sculpture, 15th century. Drawing by the authors.
6. Mother and child. 19th century, Mali, Bougouni district: Bambara. Wood. 48⅝ inches. Courtesy of the Metropolitan Museum of Art, the Michael C. Rockefeller Memorial Collection of Primitive Art.
7. *The Blind Swimmer.* Max Ernst, 1934. Oil on canvas, 36⅜ X 29 inches. Collection, the Museum of Modern Art, New York. Gift of Mrs. Pierre Matisse and Helena Rubenstein Fund.
8. The Supreme Goddess as Void. Andhra Pradesh, India, 19th century. Projection-space for image. Brass. 9 inches. Photograph courtesy of Jeffrey Teasdale. Collection of Ajit Mookerjee.
9. Lithograph. Joan Miró. Courtesy of Suzy Locke.
10. Terrible Goddess seated in intercourse on the male corpse-Shiva. Rajasthan, India, 18th century. Brass. 5 inches. Photograph courtesy of Jeffrey Teasdale. Collection of Ajit Mookerjee.
11. Fuji Pilgrimage Mandala. Muromacho period, 16th century, Japan. Sengen Shrine, Shizuoka. Photograph courtesy of the Bunkacho, Agency for Cultural Affairs of the Ministry of Education, Tokyo.
12. Chakrasamvara. Tibet, ca. 17th century. Gilt bronze. H: 12 inches. W: 10 inches. Courtesy of the Asian Art Museum of San Francisco, the Avery Brundage Collection.
13. Bear Mother. Photograph by Eberhard Otto for "The Artist as Historian," *artscanada*, June, 1975.
14. Nautilus spiral. Courtesy of the San Francisco State University Slide Library.
15. *The Coronation of the Virgin.* Paolo Veneziano, active 1324-1358. Photograph courtesy of Samuel H. Kress Collection, National Galley of Art, Washington, D.C.
16. Prince and lady prolonging their intercourse. Panjab Hills, India, 18th century. Album miniature, Kangra style. Photograph courtesy of the Victoria and Albert Museum.
17. Wooden headrest of male and female figures. Luba, Congo. Photograph courtesy of the Trustees of the British Museum.
18. Drawing by the authors.
19. 11.1 Millimeter human embryo at the end of the sixth week of development. Photograph from Dr. E Bleckschmidt. From *Die pranatalen Organsysteme des Menschen*. Stuttgart: Hippokrates, 1973.
20. *Black Abstraction.* Georgia O'Keeffe, 1927. Oil on canvas. 30 X 40¼ inches. Courtesy of Georgia O'Keeffe. Photograph courtesy of the Metropolitan Museum of Art, the Alfred Steiglitz Collection.
21. *Enso.* Torei Enji. Japan, 18th century. Collection of Dr. Kurt Gitter. Photograph courtesy of Otto Nelson.
22. Isis-Hathor suckling Horus. Egypt, 8th-6th century B.C. Bronze. Courtesy of the Louvre Museum.
23. Buffalo's head. Australian Aborigine. Liverpool River Region. Carved and painted wood. After Karel Kupka, *Dawn of Art*. Drawing by the authors.
24. The Terrible Goddess Kali. Kalighat, Calcutta, 20th century. Watercolor on paper 440 X 280 millimeters. Photograph courtesy of the Victoria and Albert Museum.
25. Demon Dance. Bali. Photograph courtesy of the Mansell Collection.

26. Coatlicue, Goddess of the Serpent Skirt. Aztec, 15th century. National Museum of Anthropology, Mexico City. Photograph courtesy of the Department of Documentation of Historical Monuments and Sites, Mexico.
27. Drawing by the authors.
28. Drawing by the authors.
29. Tripod pottery vase. Arkansas. After *Report of the U.S. National Museum,* Smithsonian Institution, Annual Report, 1895-1896. Drawing by the authors.
30. Buddha's footprint. After relief sculpture, Great Stupa, Amaravati, India. Drawing by the authors.
31. Drawing by the authors.
32. The sea-mother's coral tree of life. *Codex Medicus Graecus 1.* 6th century. Photograph courtesy of the Nationalbibliothek, Vienna.
33. From *The Formed Fetus.* Hieronymus Fabricus of Aquapendente, 1600.
34. Yaksi, earth spirit. After sculpture at Sanchi, India, 100 B.C. Drawing by the authors.
35. Tree of Death. Anonymous, German. 16th century. Woodcut.
36. *Crucixion.* Albrecht Dürer. Canon cut from *Opus Speciale Missarum;* Strasbourg, November 13, 1493.
37. Drawing by the authors.
38. Drawing by the authors.
39. From Dante's *Inferno.* Illustrated by Gustave Doré, 1861.
40. Lintel carving, Maori. New Zealand 71.19.2. Photograph courtesy of the Fine Arts Museum of San Francisco.
41. Drawing by the authors.
42. Labyrinth engraved on an ancient gem. Graeco-Roman.
43. Mahāvidyā Cinnamastā. Rajasthan, India, 18th century. Gouache on paper. 12 X 8 inches. Photograph courtesy of Jeffrey Teasdale. Collection of Ajit Mookerjee.
44. *Snake.* Watling or the Port Jackson Painter, 1790. Watercolor. Photograph courtesy of the Trustees of the British Museum of Natural History.
45. "Reclining upon a bed was a princess of radiant beauty." Gustave Doré, from *The Sleeping Beauty,* in *Les Contes de Perrault,* 1867.
46. *Knight's Dream.* Moritz von Schwind, 1822. Photograph courtesy of Rostock, Kunsthalle.
47. Uta Makura. Utamaro, 1788. Woodcut from *Pillow Poem.* Photograph courtesy of Tom Evans.
48. Queen Dedes as Prajnaparamita. Singasari, Java, late 13th century. Photograph courtesy of Rijksmuseum voor Volkenkunde, Leiden.
49. Clouds off Baja. Photograph courtesy of NASA.
50. Caddoon pottery water bottle. From Quachita parish, Louisiana, ca. 1300-1700. Drawing by the authors.
51. Dakini. Nepal, 17th-18th century. Gilt bronze. H: 7¼ inches. W: 5 inches. Courtesy of the Asian Art Museum of San Francisco, the Avery Brundage Collection.
52. The Monster of Gilgamesh Epic. Khumbaba, ca. 3000 B.C. Human placenta showing elongated umbilical cord rooted at center of nose. Drawing by the authors.
53. Emblema XLII, from *Atalanta Fugiens.* Michael Maier, Frankfort, 1617.
54. Colossal head. Olmec Culture, Mexico, ca. 1000 B.C. Basalt. Museo-Parque de la Venta, Villahermosa, Tabasco, Mexico. Photograph courtesy of the Department of Documentation of Historical Monuments and Sites, Mexico.
55. Goddess in mouth of cave. Olmec, Mexico, ca. 800 B.C. Drawing by the authors.
56. Birthgiving goddess engraved on potsherd. Northeast Hungary, ca. 5000 B.C. Drawing by the authors.
57. Mistress of the animals. 700 B.C. Greek amphora. Drawing by the authors.
58. Birthgiving Goddess in shape of toad. Bohemia, ca. 5000 B.C. Drawing by the authors.
59. Samarran pottery design. Mesopotamia, 5000-4000 B.C. After Beatrice Laura Goff, *Symbols of Prehistoric Mesopotamia.* Drawing by the authors.
60. Catal Hüyük shrine. Turkey, ca. 6000 B.C. Drawing by the authors.
61. Nut. Egypt. Sarcophagus relief.
62. Mayan Time Bearer. Drawing by the authors.
63. Offering by King Trajanus Germanicus to Hathor and Harsemtawi. Temple Denderah, Egypt. Photograph by Fred Stross.
64. World deluge presided over by the Old Goddess, Ixchel. From the *Dresden* Codex. Mayan, 12th century. Drawing by the authors.
65. The Fairy Yu Nu, Daughter of Jade. Ch'ien Hsüan, 1235-90. Photograph courtesy of the Trustees of the British Museum.
66. Figurine of Middle Jomon Period, Japan. From Chojagahara, Ichinomiya, Itoigawa City, Niigata prefecture. The Tokyo National Museum. Photograph courtesy of the Zauho Press.
67. Shinto Female Deity. Early Heian period, 9th century, Japan. Matsuno-o Shrine, Kyoto. Photograph courtesy of the Bunkacho, Agency for Cultural Affairs of the Ministry of Education, Tokyo.
68. Dagoba. Anuradhapura, Ceylon, 100 B.C. Drawing by the authors.
69. Tissamaharama. Ceylon. Photograph courtesy of Jonathan S. Hill.
70. Tibetan chöten. Drawing by the authors.
71. Hagia Sophia. Istanbul, Turkey, 19th century. Lithograph by the Fossati Brothers. The Avery Library Collection, Columbia University. Photograph courtesy of Raymond Lifchez.
72. Central dome of the Mihrumah Sultan Mosque. Üsküdar, Turkey, 1548. Photograph courtesy of Raymond Lifchez.
73. Amiens Cathedral. France, ca. 1220. Interior of nave. Photograph courtesy of Marburg Foto.
74. *The Virgin in Glory.* Albrecht Dürer. Woodcut. Title page to *The Life of the Virgin,* 1511.
75. Proposal for Sir Isaac Newton's tomb. Etienne-Louis Boullée. Photograph courtesy of the Bibliotheque Nationale, Paris.
76. *Spirit of the Dead Watching.* Paul Gauguin, 1892. Photograph courtesy of the Albright-Knox Gallery, Buffalo, New York. A. Conger Goodyear Collection.
77. Yaksi or Salabhanjika. Konarak, Orissa, India. Eastern Ganga dynasty, mid-13th century. Ferruginous sandstone. H: 48 inches. W: 13½ inches. Courtesy of the Asian Art Museum of San Francisco, the Avery Brundage Collection.

78. After German Expressionist drawing. Ca. 1915. Drawing by the authors.
79. *Madonna*. Edvard Munch, 1895. Lithograph printed in black. Photograph courtesy of the Art Institute of Chicago.
80. *Dancing Skeleton*. José Posada, ca. 1910. Woodcut.
81. Drepanocytes. Sickle cell anemia from corpuscles. Dr. Marcel Bessis, New York, 1974. Microphotograph courtesy of Dr. Marcel Bessis.
82. Bodhisattva. Khmer Civilization, Cambodia, 12th century. Sculpture. Photograph by Wim Swan. Musée Guimet, Paris.
83. *The Ballantine*. Franz Kline, 1948-1960. Oil on canvas. 72 X 72 inches. Photograph courtesy of the Los Angeles County Museum of Art. The Estate of David E. Bright.
84. Face of a 12 millimeter human embryo. Approximately 40 days. Photograph from Dr. E. Blechschmidt. *The Stages of Human Development before Birth*. Philadelphia: Saunders, 1961.
85. Wheel of Life (Bhavacakra). Tibet, 19th century. Photograph courtesy of Museum voor land en Volkenkunde, Rotterdam.
86. *Magnolia Blossom*. Imogen Cunningham, 1925. Photograph courtesy of the Imogen Cunningham Trust.
87. Olmec Priest with Jaguar Boy. Mexico, ca. 1000 B.C. (Olmec Period). Jade. Height: 8⅝ inches. Mexico. Courtesy of the Brooklyn Museum, New York.
88. *The Great Red Dragon and the Woman Clothed with the Sun*. William Blake, 19th century. Photograph courtesy of the National Galley of Art, Washington, D.C. The Rosenwald Collection.
89. The Olympic Mountains from Hurricane Ridge, Washington. Photograph by Don Worth. Courtesy of the artist.
90. Nyoirin-Kannon. (Bodhisattva of Compassion). Japan, late Heian, 900-950. Wood with coating of dry lacquer, gilt and pigments. H: 25⅞ inches. W: 20¼ inches. Courtesy of the Asian Art Museum of San Francisco, the Avery Brundage Collection.
91. Head of St. John the Baptist. Chartres, France. Photograph by Pierre Belzeaux. Courtesy of the Zodiaque Press.
92. Uni and his wife, Amen-Re. Egypt, XIX dynasty. Limestone. Photograph courtesy of the Metropolitan Museum of Art, the Rogers Fund, 1915.
93. Martha Graham — Letter to the World. Photograph by Barbara Morgan, 1940. Photograph courtesy of the Helen Foresman Spencer Museum of Art. University of Kansas, Lawrence.
94. *Starry Vault of the Queen of Night*. Karl Friedrich Schinkel, 1815. Photograph courtesy of the National Gallery, Berlin.
95. *Vampire*. Edvard Munch, 1894, Drypoint. Photograph courtesy of the Art Institute of Chicago, the Kate S. Buckingham Fund.
96. Dancing Apsaras. Cambodia, 9th-12th century. Bronze. Ross Collection 22.686. Courtesy of the Museum of Fine Arts, Boston.
97. Calligraphy. Chögyam Trungpa. Reproduced by special arrangement with Chögyam Trungpa.
98-101. Drawings by the authors.

Front Cover: The Trifid Nebula in Sagittarius. Photograph courtesy of the Lick Observatory.
Frontispiece: Fertility Goddess. Mexico, Totonac culture, 10th century. Photograph by Gisele Freund. Collection of Dr. K. Stavenhagen, Mexico. Courtesy of Magnum Photos, Inc.